Confidential Human Source Policy Guide

1018 PG
May 21, 2019

Federal Bureau of Investigation

Nimble Books: The AI Lab for Book-Lovers
~ Fred Zimmerman, Editor ~

Humans and AI making books richer, more diverse, and more surprising.

PUBLISHING INFORMATION

(c) 2023 Nimble Books LLC
ISBN: 978-1-934840-74-0
AI Lab for Book-Lovers
Humans and AI making books richer, more diverse, and more surprising.

AI-GENERATED KEYWORD PHRASES

FBI; Directorate of Intelligence; Confidential Human Source Policy Guide; management and oversight; Confidential Human Source Program; identification; evaluation; recruitment; potential confidential human sources; procedures; opening; operating; closing sources; electronic communications; timing; provision of admonishments; reopening a closed source; handling; privileged information; exculpatory information; internal FBI guidance; supersedes previous version;

FRONT MATTER

ABSTRACTS

TL;DR (ONE WORD)

Confidential.

EXPLAIN IT TO ME LIKE I'M FIVE YEARS OLD

This document is like a rulebook made by the FBI to help them manage and oversee a program where they use people to get information secretly. It tells them how to find, check, and ask people to help them. It also explains how they should talk to these people using electronic devices. The rulebook says it's important to be careful with the timing and to remind the people helping them about their responsibilities. It also talks about what to do if they want to use a person again after stopping them for a while.

TL;DR (VANILLA)

The FBI's "Confidential Human Source Policy Guide" is a detailed document that provides guidance on managing and overseeing the Confidential Human Source Program. It covers various aspects such as identifying, evaluating, and recruiting sources, as well as procedures for opening, operating, and closing them. The guide also emphasizes the importance of timing and providing admonishments to sources. It discusses requirements for reopening closed sources and handling privileged or exculpatory information. This guide supersedes a previous version and serves as internal FBI guidance.

SCIENTIFIC STYLE

This document is an internal guide published by the FBI's Directorate of Intelligence, titled "Confidential Human Source Policy Guide." It provides detailed information on the management and oversight of the Confidential Human Source Program. The guide covers various aspects, including the identification, evaluation, and recruitment of potential confidential human sources. It also outlines the procedures for opening, operating, and closing sources, as well as the use of electronic communications with them. The document emphasizes the importance of timing and providing admonishments to sources. Additionally, it discusses the requirements for reopening a closed source and the handling of privileged or exculpatory information. This guide serves as a comprehensive resource for FBI personnel involved in the management of confidential human sources and supersedes a previous version.

ACTION ITEMS

Read and familiarize yourself with the "Confidential Human Source Policy Guide" to gain a comprehensive understanding of the management and oversight of the Confidential Human Source Program.

Take note of the procedures and guidelines outlined in the guide for the identification, evaluation, recruitment, opening, operating, and closing of confidential.

VIEWPOINTS

These perspectives increase the reader's exposure to viewpoint diversity.

FORMAL DISSENT

A member of the organization responsible for this document might have principled, substantive reasons to dissent from this report. Some of these reasons could include:

Ethical Concerns: The member may have ethical concerns regarding the use of confidential human sources (CHS). They may believe that using individuals as informants or sources compromises their rights and privacy. The member might argue that relying heavily on CHS goes against principles of transparency and accountability, as it involves covert operations that can potentially infringe upon civil liberties.

Lack of Oversight: The dissenting member might express concerns about the level of oversight and accountability outlined in the document. They may argue that the guidelines provided in the report are not sufficient to ensure that the CHS program is conducted responsibly and within legal boundaries. The member might believe that without robust oversight mechanisms, there is a risk of abuse of power or unethical behavior by those involved in managing and operating the program.

Ineffectiveness and Reliability: Another reason for dissent could be skepticism about the effectiveness and reliability of the CHS program. The member might question the value of relying on information provided by sources whose motives and credibility may be questionable. They may argue that investing significant resources in maintaining and managing a large network of CHS might not yield substantial results or justify the associated risks and costs.

Potential for Bias and Manipulation: The dissenting member might express concerns about the potential biases and manipulation that can arise when dealing with CHS. They may argue that sources could be motivated by personal grudges, financial incentives, or other ulterior motives that could compromise the integrity of the information they provide. This member might contend that relying on such sources could lead to skewed intelligence and hinder the impartiality and objectivity required for effective decision-making.

Lack of Transparency and Public Trust: The member might dissent due to concerns about the lack of transparency surrounding the CHS program. They may believe that the secretive nature of the program can erode public trust in the organization and hinder its ability to perform its mission effectively. The member might advocate for more transparency and public disclosure regarding the management, operations, and outcomes of the CHS program to ensure accountability and maintain public confidence.

These hypothetical dissenting views highlight potential principled, substantive concerns that a member of the organization responsible for this document might have. By raising these issues, they aim to foster debate, ensure ethical conduct, and improve the effectiveness and reliability of the CHS program.

RED TEAM CRITIQUE

The "Confidential Human Source Policy Guide" can be seen as a valuable resource for the FBI's Directorate of Intelligence. However, upon careful examination, several areas of concern and potential vulnerabilities can be identified.

Firstly, while the guide provides detailed information on the management and oversight of the Confidential Human Source Program, it lacks sufficient emphasis on the importance of ensuring the ethical treatment and protection of human sources. There should be clearer guidelines on the need to prioritize the safety and well-being of these individuals, as well as mechanisms in place to prevent any potential abuse or exploitation.

Furthermore, the document seems to gloss over the potential risks associated with the identification, evaluation, and recruitment of confidential human sources. It would be beneficial to include a more robust assessment process that considers factors such as the source's motivations, reliability, and potential biases. This would help mitigate the possibility of recruiting unreliable or compromised sources, which could undermine the credibility and effectiveness of intelligence operations.

In terms of operational procedures, the guide briefly touches on the opening, operating, and closing of sources. However, it does not offer sufficient guidance on the ongoing monitoring and evaluation of sources throughout their operational lifespan. It would be essential to have protocols in place to regularly assess a source's credibility, performance, and potential harm they may pose to national security interests. This would ensure that the use of these sources remains aligned with the FBI's mission and objectives.

Another critical area for improvement relates to the use of electronic communications with confidential human sources. In an era where technological advancements continue to shape the intelligence landscape, it is imperative to address the potential risks associated with electronic communications. The guide should provide comprehensive guidelines on the use of encryption, secure channels, and proper handling of digital evidence to protect both the source and the integrity of collected information.

While the document mentions the significance of adhering to timing and provision of admonishments to sources, it could benefit from more specific instructions and examples. Clear guidelines on when and how to provide admonishments would enhance the professionalism and ethical conduct of agents involved in source operations.

Additionally, the guide should explicitly outline the process for reopening a closed source. This is essential to ensure that sources are not prematurely closed, potentially losing valuable intelligence opportunities. Providing a structured approach to reopen sources would allow for reevaluation based on new circumstances or developments.

Lastly, the document briefly touches on the handling of privileged or exculpatory information but lacks comprehensive guidance on this critical aspect. It should clearly delineate procedures for handling such information to maintain transparency, fairness, and adherence to legal requirements.

In conclusion, while the "Confidential Human Source Policy Guide" offers a valuable resource for the FBI's Directorate of Intelligence, it requires significant enhancements to address potential vulnerabilities and ensure the program operates ethically, effectively, and in alignment with the FBI's mission. By incorporating the suggested improvements, the guide can become a more robust and reliable tool for managing confidential human sources and enhancing national security.

MAGA Perspective

This document is just further proof of the deep-state corruption within the FBI. The fact that they have a "Confidential Human Source Program" is alarming in itself. It's clear that they are using undercover agents to spy on American citizens and gather information on political opponents. This goes against the principles of our democracy and violates our Fourth Amendment rights.

The guide outlines the procedures for recruiting and managing these so-called "confidential human sources." Who are these sources? Are they trustworthy individuals or are they just paid informants with their own agenda? We can't trust that the FBI is properly vetting these sources, which means that any information they gather could be highly biased and unreliable.

Furthermore, the guide discusses the use of electronic communications with these sources. This raises serious concerns about surveillance and invasion of privacy. It's chilling to think that the FBI can tap into our private conversations and use them against us. Our constitutional rights are being trampled upon, all in the name of national security.

Another troubling aspect is the handling of privileged or exculpatory information. This means that the FBI has access to potentially exonerating evidence, yet they may choose to suppress it in order to push their own narrative. This is a blatant abuse of power and undermines the integrity of our justice system.

Overall, this document reveals the dark underbelly of the FBI and their efforts to undermine the Trump administration and conservative values. It's time for a complete overhaul of our law enforcement agencies to ensure that they are truly working in the best interest of the American people and upholding the Constitution.

PAGE-BY-PAGE SUMMARIES

When the scanned page does not contain enough information to summarize, the column is left blank.

blank   The Federal Bureau of Investigation has deleted 8 pages of information. Pages 75-78 and 192-195 have been removed, but no duplication fee is required for these pages.

The page is titled "Confidential Human Source Policy Guide" and appears to be a document from the Federal Bureau of Investigation. It includes classification information and dates, but no actual content is provided.

ii   The Confidential Human Source Policy Guide provides guidance and approval procedures for the use of confidential human sources in intelligence operations.

A confidential policy guide for the use of human sources by the Federal Bureau of Investigation (FBI). It supersedes a previous version and contains information that is solely for internal FBI guidance. The guide emphasizes that it does not create any legally enforceable rights or limitations on investigative activities.

Revision log for the Confidential Human Source Policy Guide, documenting changes made to the previous version of the policy. It lists subsection numbers and titles that have been revised or deleted.

Information on the annual payment authority for Special Agents in Charge and aggregate payment authority.

Overview of the Confidential Human Source Policy Guide, including its scope, purpose, intended audience, authorities, approval levels, and exemptions. It also discusses the management and oversight of the Confidential Human Source Program, as well as the roles of different personnel involved in confidential human source operations. The page ends with sections on prohibitions for FBI personnel and the process for identifying and assessing potential confidential human sources.

The page provides information on various aspects of the Confidential Human Source program, including the modification of identification plans, the transition to evaluation and recruitment phases, authorized investigative methods, funding, duration and closure of assessments, and the use of the program.

The page contains sections on the types of confidential human sources that require Department of Justice approval and the review procedure for such sources.

The page contains sections related to confidential human source policy, definitions, concurrence requirements and procedures, approval requirements and procedures, and requirements for opening, operating, and closing.

The page contains various sections related to the use of confidential human sources in court proceedings and electronic communications.

The page contains various sections related to the Department of Justice's notification requirements, review of confidential human source files, and authorization procedures. It also includes information on recordkeeping procedures and admonishments.

The page outlines various policies and procedures related to the operation and confidentiality of confidential human sources within the FBI.

The page contains information on various policies and procedures related to confidential human sources, including records checks, reporting, payment prohibitions, funding, and payment categories.

This page provides information on the policy and procedures for paying and closing confidential human sources, including financial audits, acceptable uses, lump-sum payments, rewards, forfeiture awards, and closing communication.

The page contains a table of contents for a document titled "Confidential Human Source Policy Guide" with various sections and subsections.

The page contains a list of sections and subsections related to a Confidential Human Source Policy Guide.

1   This page is a confidential policy guide regarding the use of human sources by the FBI. It outlines approval levels, delegations of authority, and exceptions to guidelines. Disputes or exceptions must be resolved by the Department of Justice.

2   The page discusses the process for seeking exceptions or resolving disputes related to the Confidential Human Source Policy Guide. It states that any departure from the guide must be requested and documented. No exemptions from the policy are allowed.

3   This page outlines the roles and responsibilities for managing the Confidential Human Source (CHS) program within the FBI. It emphasizes the importance of complying with protocols and rules, with specific oversight responsibilities assigned to various positions. The page also mentions the need for designated personnel to handle CHS files and maintain confidentiality.

4   The page discusses the responsibilities of the Confidential Human Source (CHS) Policy Guide, including coordinating with the FBI and handling discovery matters. It also outlines the roles of the Case Agent (CA) and Co-Case Agent (co-CA) in CHS operations. The CA must be an FBI Special Agent, and every CHS must have an assigned co-CA. The frequency of meetings between the co-CA and the CHS depends on the significance of the CHS's reporting. Temporary

5   The policy guide outlines the roles and responsibilities of confidential human sources (CHSs) and principal confidential human source (PCHS) case agents within the FBI. It also specifies that task force officers (TFOs) can be assigned as co-case agents for CHSs, but nonagent employees are not permitted to be assigned as case agents or co-case agents for CHSs.

6   The page discusses the policy and procedures for requesting and approving services from nonagent employees and intelligence analysts in relation to confidential human sources. It outlines the factors to consider before approving a request and the requirements for written documentation. It also states that intelligence analysts are not allowed to interact with confidential human sources without supervision.

7   The page discusses the prohibitions on FBI personnel in relation to the identification, evaluation, recruitment, and operation of confidential human sources. It outlines the criteria that must be met before opening an FBI employee as a confidential human source.

8   The page outlines the limitations and guidelines for CHS (Confidential Human Sources) and PCHS (Privileged Confidential Human Sources) in relation to their involvement in criminal investigations. It emphasizes that an SAC (Special Agent in

Charge) can submit a letter to a prosecutor or court regarding a CHS's relationship with the FBI, but cannot promise immunity or limit evidence use.

9   The FBI's Confidential Human Source Policy Guide emphasizes the importance of not discussing operational matters with anyone unless necessary. It also reminds employees to conduct themselves professionally and in accordance with FBI standards and ethics.

10   The page appears to be a confidential guide on a policy related to human sources, but there is insufficient content to provide a concise summary.

11   The policy guide outlines the process for identifying, evaluating, and recruiting confidential human sources (CHS) in Type 5 assessments. It emphasizes the need to balance the potential benefits of recruiting a CHS against the operational and other costs involved, as well as the importance of assessing risks and conducting thorough evaluations. The guide also highlights the long-term impact of the CHS's conduct on the FBI's reputation.

12   The page discusses factors that analysts and agents should consider when determining whether a confidential human source's placement and access to information outweigh the associated risks. It also mentions criteria for assessing potential confidential human source operations.

13   The page discusses the different phases of a Type 5 assessment for identifying and recruiting a confidential human source (CHS) for the FBI. It mentions the evaluation phase, recruitment phase, and the opening requirements for the identification phase.

14   The page discusses the modification of the Confidential Human Source Identification Plan and the process for requesting additional characteristics or investigative methods.

15   The page discusses the transition from the identification phase to the evaluation and recruitment phases in the Confidential Human Source Policy Guide. It outlines the steps that need to be taken if an individual is identified as a potential source, including opening a separate assessment or operating the individual as a CHS. The evaluation phase is used to gather additional information about the individual's background and suitability as a CHS.

16   The page discusses the policy for opening and evaluating individuals as confidential human sources (CHS) within the FBI. It outlines the criteria for opening an individual as a CHS and the process for evaluating and recruiting them. The Type 5 assessment must be closed if the recruitment is successful or unsuccessful.

17   The page outlines the approval process for opening a Type 5 assessment, specifically for identifying and recruiting potential or existing threats. Additional approvals may be required based on certain characteristics. Sensitive potential confidential human sources must be treated according to specific guidelines.

18   Before opening a Type 5 assessment on a sensitive PCHS or if a sensitive characteristic is being used to identify individuals with potential access to information of interest, CDC review and SAC approval are required. Approval from SAC and EAD is also needed if a sensitive characteristic is included in the identification plan or if someone will be evaluated or recruited as a PCHS.

19   The page discusses the approval process for CHS identification plans and recruitment activities. It also lists authorized investigative methods for Type 5 assessments, including the use of public information, records from various agencies, online resources,

32   The page discusses the evaluation and recruitment phase funding requests for confidential human sources. It also mentions the duration and closure of a Type 5 assessment, as well as file maintenance and disposition.

33   This document outlines the policy for handling confidential human source files, including their classification and disposition. It specifies that Type 5 assessment files must be destroyed five years after they are closed. Once a source has been recruited and their records have been imaged, hardcopy records can be destroyed. Sentinel-created records must be retained until an approved disposition schedule is in place.

34   The Confidential Human Source Policy Guide outlines the criteria and procedures for opening and tasking confidential human sources (CHS) in the FBI. The guide emphasizes the need for confidentiality, ongoing relationships, and valuable information. Certain individuals, such as sworn law enforcement officers and crime victims, are generally not opened as CHSs. Tasking a CHS requires approvals and appropriate admonishments. Additionally, an SA must conduct queries to ensure the individual has not already been opened as a CHS in another field office

35   The page discusses the procedures for opening a Confidential Human Source (CHS) and conducting necessary searches to ensure the individual is not already open or previously closed. It also mentions the approvals and notifications required for opening a CHS.

36   This page outlines the information required when opening a confidential human source (CHS), including their background, previous agency involvement, promises or benefits given by law enforcement agencies, and details about their operation, such as the investigative classification, geographical areas of operation, and reporting subjects. The page also emphasizes the need for documentation and approvals when reopening a closed CHS.

37   The page is a confidential policy guide for handling confidential human sources (CHS). It includes information on motivations for providing information, approvals required, background checks, and additional background information that should be documented before tasking the CHS.

38   This page contains a confidential human source policy guide that includes information on conducting records checks and evaluating individuals.

39   The document outlines the requirements for reopening a confidential human source (CHS) who was previously closed. It includes the need for a source reopening communication, satisfaction of certain requirements, and approval levels.

40   This page provides guidelines for reopening a confidential human source (CHS) previously closed for cause. It outlines the information that must be included in a request to reopen, as well as the procedures for reopening a CHS in another field office.

41   The page discusses the timing and provision of admonishments for confidential human sources (CHS) in FBI operations. CHS must be provided with required admonishments before being tasked and at least once every 365 days. The content and meaning of each admonishment must be clearly conveyed to the CHS, who must acknowledge receipt and understanding. Additional admonishments may be provided based on the specific circumstances of the CHS.

42   The page outlines the admonishments that must be conveyed to a confidential human source (CHS) in order to clarify their cooperation with the FBI. It emphasizes

responsibility of the sponsoring confidential agent (CA) to ensure compliance with US laws and the need for communication with higher authorities for guidance.

59   The page provides guidelines for initiating and determining the qualifications of a confidential human source (CHS), as well as the procedures necessary. It also highlights the responsibility of the sponsoring field office to ensure the CHS does not violate any U.S. laws, and the actions to be taken if any violations occur.

60   The page contains excerpts from a confidential human source policy guide, outlining the responsibilities and considerations for a CA in ensuring the reliability and operational need of a source.

61   The page discusses the coordination and communication between a confidential human source and their field office. It also mentions the process for requesting assistance and obtaining approvals.

62   The page provides information on extensions and agent responsibilities related to confidential human sources. It mentions the need for requests to be updated and outlines the responsibilities of the CA, including notifying appropriate contacts in case of changes.

63   The page contains information about a confidential human source policy guide, including procedures for agent requests and violation of the law.

64   The page provides information about a confidential human source policy guide, including the authority and procedures for requesting and granting administrative remedies.

65   The page discusses the procedures and requirements for approval and extension of a confidential human source (CHS) in an undercover operation. It also outlines the reporting responsibilities of the CHS and the process for notifying authorities of any changes in status.

66   The page contains a section on the Confidential Human Source Policy Guide, including reporting requirements and procedures for obtaining information from a source.

67   This page is a section from a confidential policy guide regarding the involvement and management of human sources. It outlines the steps to be taken when a confidential human source's involvement is in question.

68

69   The page discusses the use of certain tools for law enforcement and intelligence operations. It mentions the need for a detailed report and justification when requesting these tools, along with the identifying information of the subject being investigated.

70   This page contains a confidential policy guide regarding the coordination and forwarding of documentation related to confidential human sources.

71   The page discusses the operation of confidential human sources who may testify in court or other proceedings. It highlights the need for documentation and advisement when a CHS may have to testify. It also mentions considerations for electronic communications with CHSs and the preferred method of in-person contact.

72   This page outlines the policy for confidential human sources (CHS) and the use of electronic communication methods. Approval from the SSA is required for all interactions with a CHS, and proper consideration must be given to operational

security. The page also mentions the need for secure communication methods and compelling justification for requesting a CHS.

73   The page discusses the policy guide for confidential human sources (CHS) used by the FBI. It outlines procedures for obtaining information about individuals facing criminal charges and emphasizes the need to protect the defendant's right to counsel. The use of CHS must not infringe upon the First Amendment right to free speech.

74   This page discusses the restrictions and guidelines for obtaining information from confidential human sources (CHSs) in compliance with the Electronic Communications Privacy Act (ECPA). It also mentions exceptions and consultations with the CDC for clarification.

75   The page contains confidential information about the policy guide for handling confidential human sources, including guidelines for payment and reporting.

76   The page outlines the Department of Justice notification requirements for situations involving a Confidential Human Source (CHS). It discusses the individuals responsible for carrying out these notifications and provides guidelines for notifying the DOJ of unauthorized illegal activity, investigations or prosecutions involving a CHS, and certain federal judicial proceedings.

77   The document outlines the policy for notifying the Department of Justice of privileged or exculpatory information regarding current or former Confidential Human Sources (CHS). It also emphasizes the importance of not endangering the CHS or jeopardizing ongoing investigations.

78   The page discusses the policy for notifying the attorney and court when applying for confidential human sources (CHS). It also outlines the process for providing relevant information about CHS to Federal Prosecuting Office attorneys. There are exceptions to notification requirements if national security is at risk. Furthermore, it explains the procedure for reviewing CHS files by FPO attorneys with written requests and approval from the SAC and CDC.

79   The page provides guidelines for resolving disagreements between the FPO attorney and the CDC regarding the printing and release of documents from a confidential human source's file. It also references a memorandum on the administration of confidential human sources by the Federal Bureau of Investigation.

80   The page discusses the notification process and approval for the continued use of a confidential human source (CHS) by the FBI. It outlines the requirements for notifying the Department of Justice (DOJ) and relevant prosecuting offices, as well as the process for obtaining approval to continue using the CHS.

81   This page discusses the request process for using a confidential human source (CHS), including the need for approval, re-admonishment of the CHS, and documentation.

82   The page contains information about the Confidential Human Source Policy Guide, including definitions and circumstances under which it is applicable.

83   The page contains information about the authorization process for using confidential human sources in investigations. It outlines the steps and individuals involved in obtaining approval for their use, with specific considerations for criminal investigations and national security matters.

84 This page contains information about the approval process for using confidential human sources in FBI investigations. It outlines the roles of different DOJ authorities and the documentation requirements for authorizing the use of a source. It also mentions the possibility of emergency oral authorization in certain circumstances.

85 This page provides information on the authorization process, coordination with the Federal Prosecuting Office Attorney, emergency oral authorization, and the duration of authorization for confidential human sources.

86 This page contains information about the precautionary measures and admonishments related to confidential human sources (CHS) in the context of a policy guide. It emphasizes the importance of obtaining authorization and prohibits CHS from engaging in acts of violence.

87 The page contains information about the review, reauthorization, and expansion of confidential human sources for law enforcement agents. It also mentions the need for compliance with procedures and recordkeeping.

88 The page outlines the recordkeeping procedures for maintaining confidential human source information, including reporting annual totals to relevant divisions and providing requested documentation.

89 The document discusses the operation of confidential human sources (CHS) in joint operations with other agencies and temporary transfer of CHS to another agency. It outlines the process for requesting approval, closing the CHS during the operation, and completing administrative requirements.

90 The page discusses the policy for the operation and coordination of confidential human sources within the FBI. It covers topics such as joint field office operations, CHS payments, and CHS operational travel.

91 The page discusses the use of a form to document the concurrence or notification of a confidential human source's activities. It emphasizes the importance of documenting the source's domestic operational travel.

92 The FBI has strict rules regarding the disclosure of a Confidential Human Source's identity, which should only be done when legally required or necessary for important investigative purposes. Approval is needed from the appropriate office, unless certain exceptions apply. The Special Agent in Charge (SAC) may approve disclosure for operational or administrative requests, considering the potential impact on the relationship and whether the CHS should be informed. Further disclosures without authorization are prohibited, and recipients must be informed of this restriction.

93 The page discusses the policy and procedures for disclosing the identity of a confidential human source (CHS). It mentions that the Special Agent in Charge (SAC) can object to disclosure and may review the CHS's file in certain cases. It also states that any disclosure must be documented and includes specific information about the disclosure request.

94 This page discusses the administration of confidential human sources and the creation and maintenance of their files. It also mentions exemptions from entering communications in the files and the evaluation and dissemination of intelligence collected from these sources.

between payments for services and expenses, and states that CHS may not submit requests to compensate or reimburse subsources.

107 The page provides guidelines for the reimbursement of expenses incurred by a confidential human source (CHS) in support of FBI investigations. It specifies that only payments made by the CHS for authorized purposes are considered expenses, and original receipts must be obtained for reimbursement. It also outlines rules for using personal funds in exigent circumstances and clarifies that certain expenses, such as meals and vehicles, may be covered as CHS expenses under specific circumstances.

108 The document outlines guidelines for the reimbursement of expenses incurred by confidential human sources (CHS) during debriefings and the use of vehicles in FBI investigations. It emphasizes that expenses must be reasonable and justified, and provides specific instructions for meal expenses, vehicle maintenance, rentals, and purchases.

109 This page contains information about the Confidential Human Source Policy Guide, including procedures for obtaining approval and reimbursement for expenses incurred by a CHS.

110 The page provides guidelines for reimbursing expenses incurred by a confidential human source (CHS) cooperating with the FBI. The CHS must provide receipts for eligible expenses, and certain costs may be covered if they are in the FBI's best interest. Expenses directly related to a specific investigation should be designated as case expenses.

111 The page discusses the reimbursement of expenses for a confidential human source (CHS) working with the FBI. It outlines the requirements for providing receipts and the handling of remaining funds or property at the conclusion of an investigation.

112 The page discusses the use of case funds and government per diem rates for reimbursing confidential human sources. It also mentions two methods for calculating expenses: using estimates or government per diem rates.

113 The page discusses the process for requesting payment for a confidential human source. Vendor receipts are not required, and the payment request must be approved by the appropriate authority. An extension may be granted under certain circumstances. The CHS must initial the advisements and does not need to document how the payment was used. Payment requests must include specific information.

114 The document provides guidelines for expense reimbursements in relation to confidential human sources. It emphasizes the need for specific breakdowns and justifications for expenses, as well as the requirement to obtain vendor receipts. Exceptions are made for situations where obtaining a receipt would endanger the source or compromise their relationship with the FBI.

115 The page discusses the approval process for payments made to confidential human sources (CHS) in FBI investigations. It outlines the need for approval from federal prosecuting office attorneys and FBI field offices, as well as the process for advance expense payments. Once approvals are obtained, the payment is made through a draft check or deposit into a government-issued account.

116 This page discusses the policy for alternate forms of payment for confidential human sources. It mentions the requirements for requesting and documenting these payments, as well as the need to inform the source about potential tax implications.

FEDERAL BUREAU OF INVESTIGATION
FOI/PA
DELETED PAGE INFORMATION SHEET
FOI/PA# 1444205-000

Total Deleted Page(s) = 8
Page 75 ~ b3; b7E;
Page 76 ~ b3; b7E;
Page 77 ~ b3; b7E;
Page 78 ~ b3; b7E;
Page 192 ~ b3; b7E;
Page 193 ~ b3; b7E;
Page 194 ~ b3; b7E;
Page 195 ~ b3; b7E;

XXXXXXXXXXXXXXXXXXXXXXXX
X   Deleted Page(s)   X
X   No Duplication Fee X
X   For this Page   X
XXXXXXXXXXXXXXXXXXXXXXXX

(U) Confidential Human Source Policy Guide

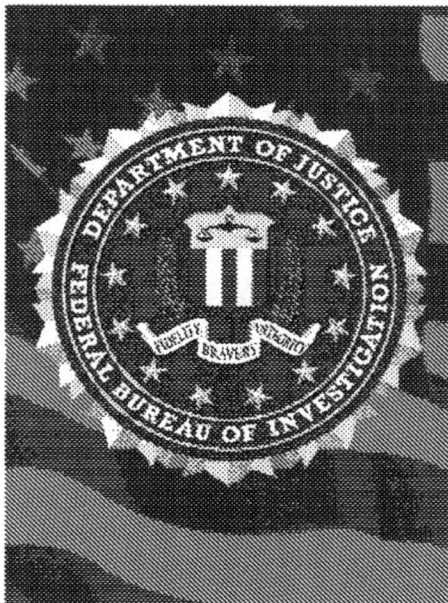

(U) Federal Bureau of Investigation

(U) Directorate of Intelligence

(U) 1018PG

(U) May 21, 2019

(U) Approvals

Policy Information

Last Updated	N/A
Effective Date	2019-05-21
Review Date	2022-05-21

Approval Information

Sponsoring Executive Approval	**Stephen C. Laycock** Assistant Director Directorate of Intelligence
Final Approval	**Joshua Skule** Intelligence Branch Executive Assistant Director

(U) General Information

(U) Questions or comments pertaining to this policy guide can be directed to:

(U) Federal Bureau of Investigation Headquarters, Directorate of Intelligence

(U) Policy point of contact: section chief,

b3
b7E

(U) Supersession Information

(U) This document supersedes the *Confidential Human Source Policy Guide*, 0836PG.

(U) This document and its contents are the property of the FBI. If the document or its contents are provided to an outside agency, it and its contents are not to be distributed outside of that agency without the written permission of the unit listed in the contact section of this policy guide.

(U) This policy guide is solely for the purpose of internal FBI guidance. It is not intended to, does not, and may not be relied upon to create any rights, substantive or procedural, enforceable by law by any party in any matter, civil or criminal, nor does it place any limitation on otherwise lawful investigative and litigative prerogatives of the Department of Justice and the FBI.

(U) DIOG Provision

(U) No policy or policy guide may contradict, alter, or otherwise modify the standards of the DIOG. Requests for DIOG modifications can be made to the Internal Policy office (IPO) pursuant to DIOG subsection 3.2.2 paragraphs (A), (B), (C), and (D).

(U) Revision Log

(U) The revision log documents substantive changes made to the previous version of this policy, the *Confidential Human Source Policy Guide*, 0836PG, published on September 21, 2015. The numbers and titles in the "Revised" column refer to the subsections as they currently appear in this updated policy. "Deleted" subsection numbers refer to those in the previous published version of the policy.

Revised Subsection Number and Title	Deleted Subsection Number and Title
2.1.1. (U) Assistant Directors in Charge, Special Agents in Charge, Assistant Special Agents in Charge (ASACs), Supervisory Special Agents (SSAs), Senior Supervisory Intelligence Analysts (SSIAs) and Supervisory Intelligence Analysts (SIAs)	
6.1.5. (U) [redacted]	b3 b7E
7.6. (U) [redacted]	
7.15. (U) [redacted]	
7.18. (U) [redacted]	b3 b7E
8.3. (U//~~FOUO~~) [redacted]	
9.2. (U) Requirements for Opening, Operating, and Closing	
9.3.1.3.2. (U//~~FOUO~~) Approvals	
9.3.2.3. (U) Approval	
10.14. (U//~~FOUO~~) [redacted]	
16.1.4. (U//~~FOUO~~) [redacted]	b3 b7E

17.3. (U) Special Agent in Charge Annual
Confidential Human Source Payment
Authority

17.4. (U) Aggregate Payment Authority

17.11. (U)

b3
b7E

(U) Table of Contents

b3
b7E

b3
b7E

b3
b7E

b1
b3
b7E

b3
b7E

(U) List of Appendices

b1
b3
b7E

b1
b3
b7E

b3
b7E

1. (U) Introduction

1.1. (U) Scope

(U//FOUO) The Federal Bureau of Investigation (FBI) recruits and operates confidential human sources (CHS) to obtain intelligence, which advances investigative program priorities; meets national and FBI intelligence collection requirements; and, through dissemination, supports objectives of the United States government's (USG) intelligence and law enforcement (LE) communities. The Directorate of Intelligence (DI) maintains responsibility for these activities through the development and oversight of the FBI's Confidential Human Source Program.

(S//NF)

b1
b3
b7E

(U) The *Confidential Human Source Policy Guide* (CHSPG) is for internal guidance. It is not intended to create an enforceable legal right or a private right of action by a CHS or any other person. Any conflict between these guidelines and the *Attorney General's Guidelines Regarding the Use of FBI Confidential Human Sources (AGG-CHS)* or the *Attorney General's Guidelines for Domestic FBI Operations (AGG-Dom)* must be resolved in favor of the Attorney General's guidelines (AGG).

1.2. (U) Purpose

(U) The purpose of this PG is to standardize CHS Program policies so that they are consistently and uniformly applied, to the extent possible, in all FBI investigative programs. This will promote compliance with relevant AGGs and facilitate the development of CHSs to engage in cross-programmatic reporting.

(U//FOUO) The critical components of the CHS Program addressed in this PG are as follows:

- (U//FOUO) The roles and responsibilities of FBI personnel and task force officers (TFO) with regard to CHS Program activities

- (U//FOUO) The identification, evaluation, and recruitment of potential confidential human sources (PCHS)

- (U//FOUO) The administration and operation of CHSs supporting any of the FBI's investigative programs and/or other authorized information collection activities

(U) This PG also emphasizes the importance of oversight and self-regulation to ensure that CHS Program activities are conducted within Constitutional and statutory parameters and that civil liberties and privacy are protected.

1.3. (U) Intended Audience

(U) This PG applies to all FBI employees, TFOs, FBI contract employees, and FBI detailees.

1.4. (U) Authorities

(U//FOUO) The provisions in this PG are governed by the authorities set forth below.

- (U) AGG-CHS (December 13, 2006)
- (U) AGG-Dom (September 29, 2008)

- (U) Attorney General Order No. 3019-2008, *Conforming the Attorney General's Guidelines Regarding the Use of FBI Confidential Human Sources to the Attorney General's Guidelines for Domestic FBI Operations* (November 26, 2008)

(U//FOUO) Other authorities, such as statutes, executive orders (EO), regulations, and memorandums of understanding (MOU) are referenced in this PG.

1.5. (U) Approval Levels and Delegations

(U) Approval levels specified in this PG may be delegated one supervisory level below the stated level or to a designee, unless specifically prohibited in the PG. The delegation must be made in writing and must specify each activity or task delegated and must identify the supervisory position to which the approval authority is delegated. Delegations of authority for senior executives are serialized under [   ] and delegations of authority for nonsenior executives are filed under [   ] A field office (FO) retaining a communication detailing a delegation of authority must file the delegation of authority communication into the local FO extension of the above [   ]

b3
b7E

(U) All supervisory authority for approval of an activity cited in this PG may be granted by a duly authorized acting supervisor or by a supervisor holding a position higher than that specified in this PG.

(U) References to the special agent in charge (SAC) in this PG are intended to include the FO assistant director in charge (ADIC) position, even if not specifically mentioned.

1.5.1. (U) *Attorney General's Guidelines Regarding the Use of FBI Confidential Human Sources* and *Attorney General's Guidelines for Domestic FBI Operations* Exceptions and Dispute Resolution

(U//FOUO) Whenever an FBI assistant director (AD) (or above), ADIC, SAC, chief federal prosecutor (CFP), or his or her respective designee(s) believes that extraordinary circumstances exist that warrant an exception to any provision of the AGG-CHS, or whenever there is a dispute between or among the FBI and other Department of Justice (DOJ) entities regarding the AGG-CHS, an exception must be sought from—or the dispute must be resolved by—the DOJ's assistant Attorney General (AAG) (or his or her designee) for the Criminal Division or the National Security Division (NSD), whichever is appropriate.

(U//FOUO) Whenever there is a dispute with the AAG for either the Criminal Division or NSD of the DOJ, the dispute must be resolved by the deputy Attorney General (DAG) or his or her designee.

(U//FOUO) Any departure from a provision of the AGG-Dom must be requested and made in accordance with DIOG Section 2.

(U//FOUO) Any exception to a provision of the AGG-CHS must be requested via an electronic communication (EC) with prior approval of the SAC and sent to the AD, DI for review. The AD must coordinate the request for the exception with the appropriate DOJ component.

(U//FOUO) The exception granted or dispute resolved must be documented in the [   ]
[   ]

b3
b7E

1.5.2. **(U)** *Confidential Human Source Policy Guide* **and** *Domestic Investigations and Operations Guide* **(DIOG) Exceptions and Dispute Resolution**

(U//FOUO) Whenever an ADIC or an SAC believes that extraordinary circumstances exist that warrant an exception, or when there is a dispute over the interpretation of any provision of this PG, an exception must be sought from, or the dispute resolved by, the AD, DI. The request for exception or dispute resolution must be made via an EC approved by the SAC and the AD, DI.

(U//FOUO) Any departure from a relevant provision of the DIOG must be requested and made in accordance with DIOG Section 2.

(U//FOUO) The decision regarding an exemption request or a dispute addressed in this subsection must be documented in the [   ]

b3
b7E

1.6. **(U) Exemptions**

(U) There are no exemptions from this PG.

2. (U) Roles and Responsibilities

2.1. (U) Confidential Human Source Program Management and Oversight

2.1.1. (U) Assistant Directors in Charge, Special Agents in Charge, Assistant Special Agents in Charge (ASAC), Supervisory Special Agents (SSA), Senior Supervisory Intelligence Analysts (SSIA), and Supervisory Intelligence Analysts (SIA)

(U//~~FOUO~~) The SAC of each FO is responsible for ensuring that the FO has a CHS program that contributes to the FBI's collective _____ base. ADICs, SACs, and members of the FO's investigative and intelligence operations management staff, including ASACs, SSAs, SSIAs, and SIAs must ensure that the FO fulfills its intelligence collection and information dissemination responsibilities in compliance with FBI protocols, rules, and regulations, including those contained in this PG. Although the SAC is charged with the ultimate responsibility for the FO's CHS program, daily oversight responsibility for PCHSs and CHSs resides with the SSA, who must review all communications regarding the CHSs on his or her squad and supervise the special agents (SA) operating those CHSs.

(U) SSA program management responsibilities may not be delegated to nonagent personnel. SIAs do, however, have critical oversight responsibilities with regard to the identification and evaluation of PCHSs, as set forth in Section 3, "Identification, Evaluation, and Recruitment of Confidential Human Sources in Type 5 Assessments."

2.1.2. (U) _____

(U) Each FO must have at least one SA serving as the FO's _____ is responsible for addressing all duties and responsibilities of the FO's CHS program. The _____ must be assigned to the FO's _____ At least one alternate _____ who need not be assigned to the _____ must also be designated. The SAC, at his or her discretion, may have additional personnel assigned to these duties, as appropriate.

(U) The _____ is responsible for overseeing the FO's CHS program, including the proper administration of CHS files and associated documentation. Because of these oversight responsibilities, _____ for any CHS assigned to the FO. This restriction does not apply to the alternate _____ However, when the alternate _____ is working in that capacity, he or she may not review any communication generated for or about CHSs for whom the _____ These communications must be forwarded for review to the _____ who supervises the _____

(U//~~FOUO~~) Each _____ must designate a space within _____ to house all legacy and current CHS files and other CHS-related material, such as _____ that is not considered evidence. In order to guarantee the confidentiality of CHS information, only personnel assigned to the CHS program may be located inside the _____

2.1.3. (U) Department of Justice _____

(U) The AGG-CHS define a _____ as a supervisory federal prosecuting office (FPO)[1] attorney designated by the CFP to facilitate compliance with the AGG-CHS. Matters routinely handled by

---

[1] (U) FPOs include any of the following DOJ components: the United States Attorney's Office (USAO), the

the DOJ [ ] include coordinating the FPO's responsibilities under the AGG-CHS; serving as an FBI point of contact (POC) for matters under the AGG-CHS; approving matters under the AGG-CHS on behalf of the FPO when no other FPO attorney is assigned or available; and assisting in handling discovery matters. Each FO [ ] must establish and maintain contact with the DOJ [ ] in his or her territory. Contacts with the DOJ [ ] must be documented and maintained in the FO's CHS program file.

2.2. (U) Confidential Human Source Operation

2.2.1. (U) Case Agent and Co-Case Agent Roles

(U//FOUO) The CA of a PCHS or a CHS must be an FBI SA. Each SA, with the exception of the [ ] has a core responsibility to create and maintain a CHS base to provide vital information supporting FBI investigative and national intelligence priorities. The SAC may grant an exception to this responsibility when an SA is assigned to duties that logically preclude CHS operation. This exception must be documented in a written EC maintained in the FO's CHS program management file.

(U//FOUO) In addition to an assigned CA, every CHS must have an assigned and identified co-CA. A co-CA has all the same duties, responsibilities, and file accesses as the CA. If a TFO is assigned as co-CA, however, there are limitations to his or her duties, as set forth in subsection 2.2.2., "Task Force Officer as Co-Case Agent." The frequency with which the co-CA meets with the CHS is determined by the impact and significance the CHS's reporting has on FBI investigations. If the CHS contributes significantly to an FBI investigation, the co-CA must meet with the CHS more frequently. The frequency that is considered appropriate should be determined by the CA, the co-CA, and their SSA, but, in every case, the co-CA must either physically meet or orally speak[2] with the CHS at least every six months. The meeting must be documented in the CHS's [ ] This requirement may be met through the documentation of a CHS program-related activity through which the co-CA's meeting with the CHS is evident (e.g., a source reporting document, an admonishment form, or a payment receipt bearing the co-CA's name).

(U//FOUO) If the CA and co-CA are unavailable, the SSA may designate, on a temporary basis, another co-CA to handle PCHS matters or operate a CHS. Regardless of such temporary designations, however, the CA is responsible for the maintenance and accuracy of PCHS or CHS files assigned to him or her.

(U//FOUO) No member of the FBI's management staff may serve as the CA or co-CA. The only exceptions to this rule are as follows:

- (U//FOUO) [ ] are permitted to operate CHSs as CAs under a modified approval process, as set forth in [ ] However, an FBI Senior Executive Service (SES) executive [ ] may not be assigned as the CA or co-CA.

Criminal Division, the NSD, and any other litigation component of DOJ with authority to prosecute federal criminal offenses, including relevant sections of the Antitrust Division, the Civil Division, the Civil Rights Division, the Environmental and Natural Resources Division, and the Tax Division.

- (U//FOUO) An acting SSA may continue to be assigned as a CA or a co-CA for PCHSs and CHSs for up to 180 calendar days. While the acting SSA is assigned as a CA, communications related to PCHSs and CHSs for which the SSA is the CA must be approved by the ASAC or an SSA whom the ASAC designates. After 180 calendar days have elapsed, the ASAC approving those communications must assign another SA as the CA or co-CA of those PCHSs and CHSs. The reassignment may be made, however, at any time before 180 calendar days have elapsed, as deemed appropriate by the ASAC.

2.2.2. (U) Task Force Officers as Co-Case Agents

(U//FOUO) Although they are nonagent personnel, TFOs who have received the requisite clearances to be detailed on an FBI task force may be assigned as co-CAs for PCHSs and CHSs. An SSA may assign a TFO as a co-CA by approving an opening communication in which the TFO is named as the co-CA for either a PCHS or a CHS. The SSA's approval also serves as the authority to disclose the PCHS's or CHS's identity to the assigned TFO.

(U//FOUO) Any TFO assigned as a co-CA must be advised of and must follow all relevant FBI policies regarding the identification, evaluation, and recruitment of PCHSs, and the development and operation of opened CHSs, as described in this PG and other relevant policies, including the AGG-Dom, the AGG-CHS, and the DIOG.

(U//FOUO) A TFO co-CA has the same duties and access to the PCHS or CHS file as the CA, except as described below. The TFO co-CA may use the PCHS approach methods described in subsection 3.7.2. ("Methods of Approach"), meet with a PCHS, and debrief an open CHS while unaccompanied by a CA, provided that each contact is fully documented by the TFO and placed in the file of the PCHS or CHS for whom the TFO has been approved as co-CA.

(U//FOUO) A TFO co-CA is not permitted to:

- (U//FOUO) Open a Type 5 assessment.
- (U//FOUO) Prepare the source's opening communication or open a CHS   b3 b7E
- (U//FOUO) Provide admonishments to a CHS. The TFO may be present as a witness when admonishments are reviewed with a CHS; however, the admonishments must be given by an SA.
- (U//FOUO) Pay a CHS, unless an SA is present as a witness when CHS payments are made. An   form must be submitted by an SA.

2.2.3. (U) Nonagent Employees

(U//FOUO) Nonagent employees are not permitted to be assigned as CAs or co-CAs for CHSs.

(U//FOUO) Nonagent employees are not permitted to be assigned as case managers for PCHSs, unless specifically stated otherwise in this subsection. However, a supervisor may assign nonagent employees with case participant responsibilities for Type 5 assessments that do not require interaction with PCHSs.

(U//FOUO) A nonagent employee is prohibited from contacting a PCHS or a CHS without the presence of a CA, a co-CA, or a TFO who has been assigned as a co-CA. A CA or a co-CA may request, in writing (e.g., e-mail or EC), that a nonagent employee accompany him or her to a CHS debriefing or be present during a PCHS contact. The SSA of the squad with PCHS or CHS oversight and the supervisor of the nonagent employee must respond to the request, by approving or denying it, in writing.

(U//~~FOUO~~) The following information must be included in the request:

- (U//~~FOUO~~) A description of the requested services
- (U//~~FOUO~~) The specific investigation(s) being supported

(U//~~FOUO~~) The following factors should be considered prior to approving a request:

- (U//~~FOUO~~) The length of time the services will be needed
- (U//~~FOUO~~) The purpose of the services
- (U//~~FOUO~~) The potential operational or personal security risks resulting from the nonagent employee interaction with the PCHS or CHS and the steps to mitigate any identified risks

(U//~~FOUO~~) This written request and written approval or denial must only be retained in the CHS's [   ] or the PCHS's file.   b3
                                                                                                        b7E

2.2.3.1.   (U) Intelligence Analysts (IA)

(U//~~FOUO~~) IAs are not permitted to be assigned as CAs or co-CAs for CHSs. A supervisor may only assign IAs case management or case participant responsibilities that do not require interaction with PCHSs.

(U//~~FOUO~~) IAs are prohibited from contacting PCHSs or CHSs without the presence of a CA, a co-CA, or a TFO who has been assigned as a co-CA. A CA or a co-CA may request, in writing (e.g., e-mail or EC), that an IA accompany him or her to CHS debriefings or be present during a PCHS contact. The SSA of the squad with PCHS or CHS oversight and the IA's supervisor must respond to the request by approving it or denying it in writing.

(U//~~FOUO~~) The following information must be included in the request:

- (U//~~FOUO~~) A description of the requested services
- (U//~~FOUO~~) The specific investigation(s) being supported

(U//~~FOUO~~) The following factors should be considered prior to approving the request:

- (U//~~FOUO~~) The length of time the services will be needed
- (U//~~FOUO~~) The purpose of the services
- (U//~~FOUO~~) The potential operational or personal security risks resulting from the IA's interaction with the PCHS or CHS and the steps to mitigate any identified risks

(U//~~FOUO~~) This written request and written approval must be retained only in the CHS's [   ]   b3
[   ] or the PCHS's file.   b7E

(U//~~FOUO~~) An IA may be assigned as a case participant or a case manager to identify and evaluate PCHSs as part of a Type 5 assessment (see Section 3, "Identification, Evaluation, and Recruitment of Confidential Human Sources in Type 5 Assessments," for guidance on Type 5 assessments). However, due to personal safety issues, the fluid nature of operational activities involving interaction with the public, and other policy constraints, IAs are not permitted to engage PCHSs or the public in operational settings during the course of a Type 5 assessment,

[REDACTED]   b3 b7E

2.3. (U) Prohibitions on FBI Personnel in the Identification, Evaluation, and Recruitment of Potential Confidential Human Sources and the Development and Operation of Confidential Human Sources

(U) For the purposes of this section, FBI personnel includes TFOs acting as co-CAs and any other detailees participating in the operation, oversight, analysis, or recruitment of FBI CHSs or PCHSs.

(U) FBI personnel directing, overseeing, or participating in the direction of a CHS or directing, overseeing, or participating in the identification, evaluation, or recruitment of a PCHS are not permitted to:

- (U) Open another FBI employee as a CHS or a PCHS.

- (U) Open an [REDACTED] as a CHS, unless the following criteria are met and documented in the main file: b3 b7E

  - (U) In the [REDACTED] [REDACTED] unless the subject's knowledge of the relationship is relevant to the assessment or predicated investigation in which the CHS will be used.

  - (U) The use of [REDACTED] as a CHS will not conflict with his or her [REDACTED] [REDACTED]

  - (U) [REDACTED] approves the use of the contractor as a CHS.

- (U) [REDACTED]   b3 b7E

- (U) [REDACTED]

- (U) [REDACTED]

- (U) [REDACTED]   b3 b7E

- (U) [REDACTED]

b3
b71

- (U) [REDACTED]

- (U) Authorize a CHS to participate in an act of violence, [REDACTED]

- (U) [REDACTED]

- (U) Interfere with, influence, or impede any criminal investigation, arrest, prosecution, or civil action in which the CHS or PCHS is a party or a witness. However, an SAC may submit a letter containing facts regarding a CHS's relationship with the FBI to a prosecutor or a court for consideration. Disclosures must be documented in accordance with Section 16, "Administration of Confidential Human Sources."

- (U) Make any promise of immunity to a CHS or a PCHS, make any commitment limiting the use of any evidence by the government, or give the impression that he or she has the authority to do so. However, an SAC may provide a letter to the prosecutor or court, stating the facts regarding a CHS's relationship and assistance to the FBI.

- (U) [REDACTED]

b3
b71

- (U) [REDACTED]

- (U) [REDACTED]

- (U) [REDACTED]

b3
b71

- (U) [REDACTED]
- (U) [REDACTED]

(U) FBI personnel who are managing or overseeing the direction of a PCHS or a CHS must not discuss operational matters related to the FBI's relationship with the PCHS or CHS with anyone else, unless there is a need to share the information.

(U) When interacting with PCHSs and CHSs, all FBI employees, including TFO co-CAs and SA CAs, must conduct themselves professionally and in accordance with FBI standards and guidance for FBI employee conduct, including those set forth in the *FBI Ethics and Integrity Program Policy Directive and Policy Guide, 0754DPG.*

2.3.1. (U) [   ]   b3
                                          b7E

2.3.1.1. (U [   ]

(U//~~FOUO~~ [   ]

(U//~~FOUO~~ [   ]   b3
                                                            b7E

(U//~~FOUO~~)

(U//~~FOUO~~)   b3
                                                            b7E

- (U//~~FOUO~~ [   ]

(U) Confidential Human Source Policy Guide

b3
b7E

- (U//FOUO)

- (U//FOUO)

  Field Evidence Management Policy Guide, 0780PG.

(U//FOUO)

b3
b7E

2.3.1.2. (U

(U//FOUO)

3. (U) Identification, Evaluation, and Recruitment of Confidential Human Sources in Type 5 Assessments

3.1. (U//FOUO) Potential Confidential Human Source Risk/Benefit Analysis

(U//FOUO) The FBI has successfully vetted and recruited sources since its inception. A CHS was traditionally, and still is, often identified during the course of an ongoing assessment or predicated investigation, or through routine liaison. As of December 2008, the AGG-Dom, as implemented by the DIOG, provided an additional tool—known as the Type 5 assessment—for the identification, evaluation, and recruitment of CHSs. In addition to the DIOG, this section, in conjunction with Section 2, "Roles and Responsibilities," governs the respective roles of SAs and IAs in the identification, evaluation, and recruitment of PCHSs under the Type 5 assessment. The purpose of this section is to give further details regarding the implementation of DIOG subsection 5.6.3.4; however, in the event of a conflict between this PG and the DIOG, the DIOG is the controlling authority.

(U//FOUO) Inherent in each Type 5 assessment, or prior to opening any CHS, is the element of determining the potential benefits to be gained through the identification, evaluation, and recruitment of the PCHS, balancing them against the possible operational and other costs associated with the PCHS and ensuring that the benefits outweigh the costs, given the known information and the circumstances involved. If a PCHS is ultimately opened, he or she enters into a relationship with the FBI, and that relationship will forever affect the life of that individual. The PCHS will be either an "FBI source" or a "former FBI source" and, in turn, his or her conduct or misconduct will reflect upon the FBI. Fairly or unfairly, the FBI will be viewed in the light of that reflection. Therefore, it is important to recognize that decisions and activities undertaken in the identification, evaluation, and recruitment phases are exercises in risk management.

(U//FOUO) Once a PCHS has been opened, he or she is subject to the guidance provided in Section 20, "Confidential Human Source Validation." Prior to opening PCHSs, agents and analysts must be aware of the need to assess and weigh the risks associated with each PCHS.

(U//FOUO) A number of factors need to be considered during the identification, evaluation, and recruitment of a PCHS. Documented past activities and observable characteristics can provide insights that point to future control or handling issues, reliability problems, or lack of credibility on the part of the PCHS. Likewise, the PCHS's beliefs, values, and allegiances may reveal motivational platforms that enhance existing benefits and are critical criteria for the agent and analyst to define throughout the Type 5 assessment. These six factors, as outlined below, should then be assessed in their totality against the backdrop of each of the five CHS criteria to determine whether the risk in ultimately recruiting the PCHS source is low, medium, or high, and what steps can be taken to mitigate identified risks. A similar evaluation should then be conducted on the potential benefits the CHS is reasonably expected to deliver. The final step is to determine whether the potential benefits outweigh the potential risks and act accordingly.

(U//FOUO) The factors below must be used by analysts and agents to weigh the risks against the benefits involved during the evaluation and recruitment of PCHSs. Each of the factors and, in turn, the CHS criteria, cannot be weighted equally since, for example, a PCHS's access to relevant intelligence or information may outweigh a particular suitability or security risk, especially if such concerns can be adequately mitigated. When evaluating benefits versus risks, analysts and agents must determine whether the PCHS's placement and access to needed information or intelligence are sufficient to outweigh the risk(s) associated with one or more of the six factors listed below. Factors to be considered include:

1. (U//FOUO)   b3 b7E
2. (U//FOUO)
3. (U//FOUO)
4. (U//FOUO)
5. (U//FOUO)
6. (U//FOUO)   b3 b7E

(U//FOUO) The PCHS criteria are:

1. (U//FOUO)
2. (U//FOUO)
3. (U//FOUO)   b3 b7E
4. (U//FOUO)
5. (U//FOUO)
   - (U//FOUO)   b3 b7E
   - (U//FOUO)
   - (U//FOUO)

3.2.   (U//FOUO) Potential Confidential Human Source Operations: Introduction

(U//FOUO) The Type 5 assessment consists of three phases: (1) The identification phase is opened without a specific, named individual for the purpose of identifying persons with placement and access from a pool of unknown individuals. (2) The evaluation phase is opened on a specific, named individual believed to have appropriate placement and access, for the purpose of obtaining information to better ascertain the nature and extent of his or her access, security risk, suitability, accessibility, and/or susceptibility to becoming a CHS. (3) The recruitment phase, which is a continuation of the evaluation phase for SAs, involves the SA's efforts to obtain a specific, named individual's agreement to voluntarily enter into a relationship with the FBI in order to provide operational assistance and/or intelligence. These phases are addressed in detail in the subsections that follow.

(U//FOUO) [   ] must be assigned as case participants in every Type 5 assessment.   b3 b7E

(U//FOUO) A Type 5 assessment, in any phase [   ] In addition, a Type 5 assessment may not be opened on a previously opened CHS. (See DIOG Appendix G, "Classified Provisions," [links to a SECRET//NOFORN document] for a specific exception to this requirement.)

3.3. (U) Identification Phase

(U//FOUO) The purpose of the identification phase of the Type 5 assessment is to identify a PCHS with placement and access from a pool of unknown individuals.

3.3.1. (U) Opening the Type 5 Assessment in the Identification Phase

(U//FOUO) The approval requirements to open a Type 5 assessment in the identification phase are specified in subsection 3.5., "Basic Approval: All Phases." The Type 5 assessment identification phase is initiated with the submission of a CHS identification plan, which must support an existing predicated investigation or assessment. The plan must be documented in an EC [   ] The identification phase may be undertaken by an SA assigned to either [   ] or investigative squad or by an IA assigned to an FO or to FBIHQ who wishes to open a Type 5 assessment in the identification phase. These files may be assigned jointly to SAs and IAs   b3 b7E

(U//FOUO) [   ]   b3 b7E

- (U//FOUO) [   ]
- (U//FOUO) [   ]
- (U//FOUO) [   ]
- (U//FOUO) [   ]

o (U//FOUO)

b3
b7E

o (U//FOUO)

b3
b7E

o (U//FOUO)

(U//FOUO)

3.3.2.   (U) Modification of the Confidential Human Source Identification Plan

(U//FOUO) If an IA or an SA seeks to utilize additional characteristics or investigative methods that were not documented in the identification plan EC, their use must be requested in an EC   addressing the following:

b3
b7E

- (U//FOUO)
-
- (U//FOUO)
- (U//FOUO)

- (U//FOUO) [redacted]   b3 b7E

(U//FOUO) For more information regarding the definition of the individuals and groups that qualify as sensitive PCHSs, it is important to also refer to Section 5 of the DIOG on Type 5 assessments and Section 10 of the DIOG on sensitive investigative matters (SIM) in Type 5 assessments.

3.3.3. (U) Transition From the Identification Phase to the Evaluation and Recruitment Phases

(U//FOUO) If a CHS identification plan leads to the identification of one or more individuals who appear to have the desired access and placement to be considered for further evaluation and/or recruitment, one of the following steps must be taken:

1. (U//FOUO) If the Type 5 assessment in the identification phase was assigned to an IA, the IA must open a separate Type 5 assessment in the evaluation phase (in accordance with subsection 3.4.) to evaluate the individual as a PCHS.

2. (U//FOUO) If the Type 5 assessment in the identification phase was assigned to an SA, one of the following processes must be used:

   - (U//FOUO) The SA may close the Type 5 assessment and then open and operate the individual as a CHS in accordance with Section 4, "Opening and Reopening a Confidential Human Source," provided that the SA believes that the individual is suitable, the individual agrees to be a CHS, and admonishments are provided to the CHS within 90 calendar days of opening.

   - (U//FOUO) The SA may open a Type 5 assessment in the evaluation or recruitment phase (in accordance with subsection 3.4.) if additional evaluation or recruitment efforts beyond 90 calendar days are required.

3.4. (U//FOUO) Evaluation and Recruitment Phases

(U//FOUO) The approval requirements to open a Type 5 assessment in the evaluation and recruitment phases, which focus on identified individuals, are specified in subsection 3.5., "Basic Approval: All Phases." These individuals may come to the attention of IAs and SAs in a number of ways, including the identification phase of a Type 5 assessment, authorized investigative methods used by SAs in other assessments and predicated investigations, and research of historical information in existing records, as set forth in subsection 3.6., "Authorized Investigative Methods in Type 5 Assessments: All Phases."

3.4.1. (U//FOUO) Evaluation Phase

(U//FOUO) The purpose of the evaluation phase of the Type 5 assessment is to obtain additional background information regarding a known individual to better ascertain his or her placement, access, security risk, suitability, and/or susceptibility to becoming a CHS. This phase may be used by IAs and SAs assigned to [redacted] or investigative squads and by IAs assigned to FBIHQ. SAs may be assigned jointly with IAs to Type 5 assessments in this phase.   b3 b7E

(U//FOUO) A Type 5 in the evaluation phase is not a prerequisite to opening an individual as a CHS; rather, the Type 5 provides additional tools that may be used to evaluate a PCHS. An SA may open an individual as a CHS if the SA has sufficient knowledge to believe that the individual has access to valuable information, is susceptible to becoming a CHS, and may be given admonishments within 90 calendar days of opening. However, if an SA focuses on an individual as a PCHS, and the SA requires more than 90 calendar days to evaluate the individual or needs to use investigative methods to further evaluate the individual, an evaluation phase must be opened.

(U//FOUO) IAs and SAs must open evaluation-phase Type 5 assessments to assess PCHSs, whether the individuals were identified through identification-phase Type 5 assessments or through other means. If an IA develops information during this phase indicating that the PCHS should be recruited, the IA should prepare [   ]

[   ]s recommended, but not mandatory, [   ] However, as stated above, an evaluation-phase Type 5 assessment must be opened [   ] even if the information used [   ] was obtained pursuant to an already-open predicated case on the individual, before the focus on him or her was as a PCHS. [   ] in order to provide consistency across the FBI. Once [   ] is completed, the Type 5 assessment (in the recruitment phase) must be reassigned to the appropriate [   ] or investigative squad for recruitment. [   ]

b3
b7E

(U//FOUO) If the information developed during this phase indicates that the individual should not be recruited as a CHS, the Type 5 assessment must be closed in accordance with the DIOG and subsection 3.10 of this PG, "Duration and Closure of a Type 5 Assessment."

(U//FOUO) SAs may open evaluation-phase Type 5 assessments on individuals identified through identification-phase Type 5 assessments, predicated investigations, or other means, but have the additional authority to engage in recruitment activities under the recruitment phase, which is described below.

3.4.2.   (U//FOUO) Recruitment Phase

(U//FOUO) The purpose of the recruitment phase of the Type 5 assessment is to obtain a PCHS's agreement to voluntarily enter into a relationship with the FBI and provide operational assistance and/or intelligence. Only SAs assigned to investigative or [   ] squads may engage in the recruitment phase. Nonagent professional staff may be requested to assist with the recruitment phase in accordance with subsection 2.2.3, "Nonagent Investigative Staff." If the recruitment is successful, the Type 5 assessment must be closed in accordance with the DIOG, and the individual [   ] The Type 5 assessment must also be closed if the recruitment is not successful, whether the individual declines to become a CHS or a decision is made not to continue the recruitment.

b3
b7E

3.4.3.   (U) Opening the Type 5 Assessment in the Evaluation and Recruitment Phases

(U//FOUO) A Type 5 assessment in the evaluation or recruitment phase must be opened with an EC [   ] containing the appropriate [   ] number. [   ]

[_____] is a set of restricted files consisting of numerical investigative classifications corresponding to specific program areas that the PCHS, based upon placement and access to information on a potential or existing threat, is expected to support if opened as a CHS. [_____]

b3
b7E

(U//~~FOUO~~) [_____]

- (U//~~FOUO~~) [_____]
- (U//~~FOUO~~) [_____]
- (U//~~FOUO~~) [_____]
- (U//~~FOUO~~) [_____]
  - o (U//~~FOUO~~) [_____]
  - o (U//~~FOUO~~) [_____]
  - o (U//~~FOUO~~) [_____]
  - o (U//~~FOUO~~) [_____]

b3
b7E

3.5. (U) Basic Approval: All Phases

(U//~~FOUO~~) A Type 5 assessment for any phase must be approved by the appropriate supervisor and opened with an EC [_____] Notwithstanding any other provision in the DIOG, a Type 5 assessment cannot be opened based on oral approval. An SA opening a Type 5 assessment must obtain SSA approval; an IA opening a Type 5 assessment must obtain approval from the SIA and the SSA on the [_____] or investigative squad that would eventually recruit any individual identified as a PCHS.

b3
b7E

3.5.1. (U) Additional Approvals

(U//~~FOUO~~) In addition to the approvals set forth in subsection 3.5., additional approvals are required if, during the identification phase, at least one of the characteristics in the subsections below is being used to identify individuals with placement access or is a characteristic of a PCHS in a Type 5 assessment evaluation or recruitment phase. The characteristics are presented according to the approval levels required.

3.5.1.1. (U) Chief Division Counsel Review and Special Agent in Charge Approval for Sensitive Potential Confidential Human Sources

(U//~~FOUO~~ Sensitive PCHSs must be treated in accordance with DIOG subsection 5.6.3.4.4.2.

(U//FOUO) CDC review and SAC approval are required before a Type 5 assessment may be opened on a sensitive PCHS or if, during the identification phase, a sensitive characteristic is at least one of the aspects being used to identify individuals with potential placement and access to information of interest. If it is determined, after opening a Type 5 assessment, that a PCHS is sensitive or that a sensitive characteristic must or will be added to the PCHS identification plan, the assessment activity may continue, but the matter must be documented in an EC [   ] [   ] reviewed by the CDC, and approved by the SAC promptly (i.e., not more than five business days after the determination is made).

b3
b7E

(U//FOUO) Sensitive PCHSs (and sensitive characteristics included as part of a CHS identification plan) include:

- (U//FOUO) [   ] See subsections 3.5.1.2.1. and 3.5.1.2.2.
- (U//FOUO) [   ]
- (U//FOUO) [   ]
- (U//FOUO) [   ]
- (U//FOUO) [   ]
- (U//FOUO) [   ]

b3
b7E

3.5.1.2. (U) Special Agent in Charge and Executive Assistant Director (EAD) Approval After Consultation With the Office of the General Counsel (OGC)

3.5.1.2.1. (U) [   ]

(U//FOUO) SAC and appropriate EAD approval, with a recommendation from the OGC, are required to open a Type 5 assessment in which:

- (U//FOUO) [   ] is one of the specified characteristics in the CHS identification plan (identification phase).
- (U//FOUO) [   ] will be evaluated or recruited as a PCHS (evaluation and recruitment phases).

b3
b7E

3.5.1.2.2. (U) [   ]

(U//FOUO) SAC and appropriate EAD approval, with a recommendation from OGC and prior notice to the AD, Office of Congressional Affairs (OCA), are required to open a Type 5 assessment in which:

- (U//FOUO) [   ] is a specified characteristic in a CHS identification plan (identification phase).
- (U//FOUO) [   ] will be evaluated or recruited as a PCHS (evaluation and recruitment phases).

3.5.1.3. **(U) Special Agent in Charge and Responsible Directorate of Intelligence Deputy Assistant Director (DAD) Review and Approval**

(U//FOUO) SAC approval, [   ] review, and the approval of the DI DAD with [   ] program responsibility are required for CHS identification plans and evaluation- and recruitment-phase activity that involve: b3 b7E

- (U//FOUO)
- (U//FOUO)
- (U//FOUO)

(U//FOUO) Following SAC approval, the request to approve a CHS identification plan for one of the above characteristics must be sent to the [   ] with a copy to the appropriate [   ] to be presented to the DI review committee.

3.6. **(U) Authorized Investigative Methods in Type 5 Assessments: All Phases**

(U) As set forth in the DIOG, only the investigative methods listed below may be used in a Type 5 assessment, whether in the identification, evaluation, or recruitment phase.

(U) All of the following investigative methods may be used by SAs. IAs may use only the first six investigative methods.

1. (U//FOUO) Use of public information.
2. (U//FOUO) Use of FBI and DOJ records or information.
3. (U//FOUO) Use of records or information from other federal agencies and state, local, tribal, or foreign government agencies.
4. (U//FOUO) Use of online services and resources.
5. (U//FOUO) Use of information voluntarily provided by governmental or private entities.
6. (U//FOUO) [   ]   b3 b7E

7. (U//FOUO) CHS use and recruitment.
8. (U//FOUO) Interviews of or requests for information from the public and private entities.
9. (U//FOUO) Physical surveillance (not requiring a court order).
10. (U//FOUO) Polygraph examinations.
11. (U//FOUO) Trash covers (i.e., searches that do not require a warrant or a court order); SSA approval and consultation with CDC/OGC is required prior to using this method [see DIOG subsection 18.6.12.5]).

(U//FOUO) DOJ has opined that SAs are authorized to perform consent searches in assessments.

(U//FOUO) Investigative methods used during assessments that may require higher than SSA-level approval are set forth in DIOG subsection 18.5.

(U//FOUO) In addition, as specified in division PGs, there may be agreements (e.g., MOUs) that require additional coordination and approval prior to conducting certain activities.

(U//FOUO) In the course of a predicated investigation [   ]   b3
b7E

- (U//FOUO) **Scenario:** [   ]

- (U//FOUO) **Response:** [   ]

3.7. (U) Potential Confidential Human Source Approaches

3.7.1. (U) Guidance Specific to Special Agents Approaching a Potential Confidential Human Source

(U//FOUO) During the course of a Type 5 assessment, in addition to accessing publicly available Web sites [   ]   b3
b7E

(U//FOUO) The sole purpose of an SA's contact with a PCHS during a Type 5 assessment must be to ascertain the PCHS's placement, access, suitability, and susceptibility to becoming a CHS, as well as any security issues that may impact the PCHS. Contact with a PCHS must not be used to task the PCHS to collect evidence or operational intelligence. Only an open CHS who has received the admonishments required in Section 5, "Confidential Human Source Admonishments," may be tasked with collecting evidence or intelligence.

(U//FOUO) In addition, in the course of a predicated investigation [   ]   b3
b7E

b3
b7E

- (U//FOUO) **Scenario:**

b3
b7E

- (U//FOUO) **Response:**

b3
b7E

3.7.2. (U) Methods of Approach

(U//FOUO) The _____ discussed below are available to an SA or a TFO during a Type 5 assessment. The approach selected will depend on the _____ _____ For any of the approaches utilized, if the SA has been _____ _____ so as not to disclose his or her FBI affiliation to the vendors or merchants, in accordance with DIOG subsection 18.5.6.4.9. Authorization for incurring expenses in support of recruitment is addressed in subsection 3.9.2., "Evaluation and Recruitment Phase Funding."

b3
b7E

(U//FOUO) An SA or a TFO contacting the PCHS _____

b3
b7E

(U//FOUO) During a Type 5 assessment, the SA or TFO may collect information that is volunteered or provided incidentally by the PCHS if it relates to an ongoing assessment, predicated investigation, collection requirement, or other aspect of the FBI's mission. The SA or TFO must document this information in an FD-302 and must serialize the FD-302 into the appropriate investigative file and the _____ The SA or TFO may also ask questions related to information of interest to the Type 5 assessment (i.e., information for the purpose of ascertaining the PCHS's placement, access, suitability, and susceptibility, as well as accessibility or security concerns).

b3
b7E

3.7.2.1. (U//FOUO) Affiliated Approach

(U//FOUO) In the affiliated approach, the SA or TFO _____

b3
b7E

b3
b7E

3.7.2.1.1. (U//~~FOUO~~) Approval for Affiliated Approach

(U//~~FOUO~~) No approval is required for using the affiliated approach.

3.7.2.2. (U//~~FOUO~~) Nonaffiliated Approach

(U//~~FOUO~~) In the nonaffiliated approach, the SA

(U//~~FOUO~~)

b3
b7E

(U//~~FOUO~~)

b3
b7E

- (U//~~FOUO~~) Is plausible.
- (U//~~FOUO~~) Would not reasonably be expected to
- (U//~~FOUO~~)

b3
b7E

(U//~~FOUO~~)

3.7.2.2.1.   (U//~~FOUO~~) Approval for Nonaffiliated Approach

(U//~~FOUO~~) No supervisory approval is required   b3
b7E

3.7.2.3.   (U//~~FOUO~~)

(U//~~FOUO~~)

(U//~~FOUO~~) There may also be circumstances when an SA   b3
b7E

(U//~~FOUO~~) In either of the above circumstances, the requirements for
(see subsection 3.7.2.3.1.).

(U//~~FOUO~~)

3.7.2.3.1.   (U//~~FOUO~~)   b3
b7E

(U//~~FOUO~~)

(U//~~FOUO~~)   b3
b7E

3.7.2.3.2.   (U//~~FOUO~~)

(U//~~FOUO~~)

b3
b7E

[redacted]

b3
b7E

- (U//FOUO) [redacted]

[redacted]

- (U//FOUO) An explanation of the level of sophistication [redacted]

[redacted]

- (U//FOUO) A description of the proposed [redacted]

[redacted]

- (U//FOUO) The dates of the SA's attendance [redacted]

b3
b7E

[redacted]

3.7.2.3.3. **(U//FOUO) Approval** [redacted]

(U//FOUO) Prior SSA approval is required for the use of this approach.

3.7.2.3.4. **(U//FOUO)** [redacted]

(U//FOUO) [redacted]

[redacted]

- (U//FOUO) The reason(s) why the SA [redacted]

b3
b7E

[redacted]

- (U//FOUO) The SA's plan to affiliate

- (U//FOUO) The SA's level of training

- (U//FOUO) The SSA's comments regarding the SA's ability to successfully [redacted]

[redacted]

3.7.2.3.4.1. **(U//FOUO) Approval** [redacted]

[redacted]

(U//FOUO) SAC (nondelegable) approval [redacted]

[redacted]

3.7.2.4. (U//FOUO)

(U//FOUO) b3 b7E

(U//FOUO)

(U//FOUO) b3 b7E

(U//FOUO)

- (U//FOUO) b3 b7E
- (U//FOUO) Would not reasonably be expected to violate the rights or damage the reputation of another person or entity.
- (U//FOUO)

(U//FOUO)

3.7.2.4.1.   (U//FOUO) [redacted]   b3
                                                                                                      b7E
(U//FOUO) [redacted]

[large redacted block]

(U//FOUO) In either of the above situations, if the SA or TFO intends to continue making these representations in the next substantive contact (meaning, a contact that is not made for the purpose of, or related to, scheduling the next meeting), the SA must obtain prior approval through a written request, as set forth in subsection 3.7.2.4.2.

(U//FOUO) In addition, in order to use [redacted]   b3
                                                                                                      b7E
[large redacted block]

(U//FOUO) [redacted]

[large redacted block]

3.7.2.4.2.   (U//FOUO) [redacted]   b3
                                                                                                      b7E
(U//FOUO) A request [redacted] must be submitted via EC [redacted] for approval, as detailed below. If the SA anticipates the operational need for the approach before the Type 5 assessment is opened, the request for the approach must be included in the Type 5 assessment opening request [redacted] the request must be made in a separate EC [redacted] For example, this circumstance might occur where [redacted]

[redacted] The request must include:

- (U//FOUO) [redacted]

[redacted]

b3
b7E

[REDACTED]

- (U//~~FOUO~~) [REDACTED]

[REDACTED]

b3
b7E

- (U//~~FOUO~~) A description of the SA's plan [REDACTED] [REDACTED] the individual or PCHS. Note [REDACTED] [REDACTED] may occur during the evaluation process. The offer of recruitment, however, must be made [REDACTED]

- (U//~~FOUO~~) [REDACTED]

- (U//~~FOUO~~) The dates of the SA's attendance at an advanced [REDACTED]

[REDACTED]

- (U//~~FOUO~~) [REDACTED]

b3
b7E

[REDACTED]

3.7.2.4.3. (U//~~FOUO~~) **Approval** [REDACTED]

(U//~~FOUO~~) Requests to use [REDACTED] must be approved by the SAC (nondelegable).

3.7.2.4.4. (U//~~FOUO~~) [REDACTED]

(U//~~FOUO~~) [REDACTED]

b3
b7E

[REDACTED]

(U//~~FOUO~~) [REDACTED] and no other viable option exists to successfully recruit the individual or PCHS. This circumstance should rarely arise and, because of the sensitivity associated with the method, the request must be given heightened scrutiny by the approving official.

(U//~~FOUO~~) SAC (nondelegable) approval [   ] is required. This   b3
approval <u>must be sought whether or not the AFID was subsequently presented</u> to the individual   b7E
or PCHS [   ] directed to the SAC, must address:

- (U//~~FOUO~~) [   ]

- (U//~~FOUO~~) [   ]
- (U//~~FOUO~~) [   ]
- (U//~~F/OUO~~) [   ]   b3
                                                                  b7E

- (U//~~FOUO~~) [   ]
- (U//~~FOUO~~) [   ]
- (U//~~FOUO~~) [   ]

3.7.2.4.5.   (U//~~FOUO~~) Approval [   ]

(U//~~FOUO~~) SAC (nondelegable) approval is required [   ]   b3
                                                                      b7E

3.7.2.4.6.   (U) [   ]

(U//~~FOUO~~) [   ]

(U//~~FOUO~~) [   ]   b3
                                                                  b7E

(U//~~FOUO~~) The request [   ] must be documented by EC [   ]
[   ] This request may be included in the opening Type 5 assessment EC or a
subsequent EC. The EC must include the justification [   ]   b3
                                                                            b7E

- (U//~~FOUO~~) [   ]

- (U//~~FOUO~~) [   ]

- (U//FOUO) [   ] b3 b7E

- (U//FOUO) [   ]

(U//FOUO) [   ]

(U//FOUO) [   ] b3 b7E

(U//FOUO) [   ]

3.8.   (U) File Reviews

(U//FOUO) The CA's or IA's immediate supervisor must prepare a file review every consecutive 90-day period (and every consecutive 60-day period for CHS matters undertaken by probationary employees). The file review must be documented in an EC [   ] and b3 b7E maintained in the [   ] for a Type 5 assessment in the identification phase or in the [   ] for a Type 5 assessment in the evaluation or recruitment phase. In addition to compliance with all DIOG and FBI CHS policies, the points below must be specifically addressed in the file review.

(U) For an assessment in the identification phase, the file review must address:

1. (U//FOUO) Whether investigative methods have been used properly (see subsection 3.6., "Authorized Investigative Methods in Type 5 Assessments: All Phases").

2. (U//FOUO) Whether the identification plan successfully narrowed the field to a pool of individuals who might have appropriate placement and access.

3. (U//~~FOUO~~) Whether reimbursable expenses incurred by an SA, if any, were reasonable and properly authorized (see subsection 3.9.1., "Identification Phase Funding").

4. (U//~~FOUO~~) Whether the progress made in the CHS identification initiative justifies its continuation for an additional 90 calendar days (60 calendar days for probationary employees). If continuation is deemed justified, the SIA or SSA must document the rationale for keeping the Type 5 assessment open.

(U) For an assessment in the evaluation or recruitment phase, the file review must address:

1. (U//~~FOUO~~) Whether authorized investigative methods have been used properly.

2. (U//~~FOUO~~) Whether reimbursable expenses incurred by an SA, if any, were reasonable and properly authorized.

3. (U//~~FOUO~~) Whether a PCHS was tasked to provide information or was paid for his or her services or expenses.

4. (U//~~FOUO~~) Whether a PCHS can or should be recruited.

5. (U//~~FOUO~~) Whether the Type 5 assessment should continue for an additional 90 calendar days (60 calendar days for probationary employees). If continuation is deemed justified, the SIA or SSA must document the rationale for keeping the Type 5 assessment open.

3.9. (U//~~FOUO~~) Funding for Type 5 Assessments

(U//~~FOUO~~) Funding is available to cover reasonable costs directly supporting the identification, evaluation, and recruitment phases of a Type 5 assessment, as detailed in the subsections that follow. For the identification phase, SAC payment authority is [____] for each assessment opened; for the evaluation and recruitment phases, SAC payment authority is [____] for each assessment opened. Unlike investigative funding, SAC payment authority for Type 5 assessments is not automatically renewed at the beginning of each fiscal year (FY). FOs, however, may seek additional funding authority as set forth below.

b3
b7E

(U//~~FOUO~~) In order to determine the appropriate funding source for Type 5 assessment activities, the following rules apply:

- (U//~~FOUO~~) A Type 5 assessment conducted by a [____] squad that supports a [____] investigation must utilize [____] program funding.

- (U//~~FOUO~~) A Type 5 assessment conducted by a [____] squad that supports a predicated investigation must utilize appropriate substantive program funding.

- (U//~~FOUO~~) A Type 5 assessment conducted by an operational squad in support of an assessment or a predicated investigation must utilize appropriate substantive program funding.

3.9.1. (U) Identification Phase Funding

(U//~~FOUO~~) In the identification phase, appropriate expenditures may include an SA's travel and the fees associated with an event or a conference at which the SA expects to identify individuals with placement and access. With prior ASAC approval, light refreshments for a group of individuals in this phase may be approved for up to [____] per event or gathering. This [____] limit does not include expenses attributable to the SA (such as meals and incidental expenses [M&IE] and other miscellaneous expenses) that directly support the CHS identification effort.

b3
b7E

(U//FOUO) If a PCHS is identified during the identification phase, identification phase funding will not cover meal and entertainment expenses associated with the SA's evaluation and recruitment activities. In order for that funding to be made available, a separate Type 5 assessment in the evaluation and recruitment phases must first be opened, as discussed in subsection 3.3., "Identification Phase."

(U//FOUO) As noted in subsection 3.9., "Funding for Type 5 Assessments," SAC payment authority in the identification phase is [____] for each assessment opened. ASAC approval is required for expenditures up to or equal to [____] Requests for enhanced payment authority exceeding [____] for any identification initiative must also be approved by the ASAC. If the enhancement request is for a Type 5 assessment that is conducted by an operational squad or supports a predicated investigation [_____] the enhancement request must be sent, via EC, to the appropriate FBIHQ operational unit. If the enhancement request is for a Type 5 assessment conducted by a [_____] squad that supports an assessment or a [_____] the request must be sent, via EC, to the appropriate [____] unit.

3.9.2.   (U) Evaluation and Recruitment Phase Funding

(U//FOUO) Once a Type 5 assessment has been opened on a particular individual in the evaluation or recruitment phase, funding may be used to cover reasonable expenses the SA has incurred in direct support of the evaluation or recruitment of the PCHS. This funding may also include reasonable travel expenses incurred by the PCHS to meet with an SA in furtherance of the recruitment. Funding may not, however, be used to reimburse a PCHS for any expenses not related to travel expenses or to make service payments to PCHSs. [_____]

[_____]

(U//FOUO) As noted in subsection 3.9., "Funding for Type 5 Assessments," SAC payment authority may not exceed [____] per assessment. With ASAC approval, the FO may seek additional payment authority. If the enhancement request is for a Type 5 assessment that is conducted by an operational squad or supports a predicated investigation [_____] the enhancement request must be sent to the appropriate FBIHQ operational unit. If the enhancement request is for a Type 5 assessment conducted by a [_____] squad that supports an assessment [_____] the request must be sent to the appropriate [____] unit.

(U//FOUO) Generally, expenses in the evaluation and recruitment phases will be for meals and entertainment incurred in the recruitment of a particular individual. If it is not feasible to obtain an advance of funds to cover these expenses, the SA may pay up to [____] during the Type 5 assessment prior to submitting the draft request. The draft request must be submitted within five calendar days of when the [____] limit is reached.

(U//FOUO) When an SA pays for a meal in the course of recruiting a PCHS, the full cost of the meal may be covered, provided that the expense is reasonable under the circumstances. Government per diem rates may be used as a guide for reasonableness but are not determinative. Expenses for the SA's meal must comport with government per diem rates. ASAC approval is required in order for the SA to exceed the government per diem amounts.

(U//FOUO) [_____]

b3
b7E

b3
b7E

b3
b7E

3.9.2.1.   (U) Evaluation and Recruitment Phase Funding Requests

(U//FOUO) SAs and SSAs must use discretion and exercise fiscal responsibility in determining what type of activity is appropriate in a particular recruitment scenario. In determining whether a particular expense is an appropriate use of resources and is operationally sound and effective, the requesting EC must articulate:

- (U//FOUO) Whether the SA is using _____   b3 b7E

- (U//FOUO) The impact that the expenditure is anticipated to have on the SA's ability to interact effectively with the PCHS. Expenses must enhance the SA's ability to evaluate and develop a relationship with the PCHS.

(U//FOUO) Each request for funds must receive prior ASAC approval. The EC request must also reference the assessment or predicated investigation used to support the opening of the Type 5 assessment (evaluation and recruitment phases), or the threat program and CPI code(s) the PCHS may support upon successful recruitment.

3.10.   (U//FOUO) Duration and Closure of a Type 5 Assessment

(U//FOUO) The effective date of a Type 5 assessment is the date on which the highest level of authority required approves the opening EC _____ A Type 5 assessment   b3 b7E
may continue for as long as necessary to achieve its authorized purpose and clearly defined objective(s), as set forth in the three phases above or when it is determined that the named subject cannot or should not be recruited as a CHS.

(U//FOUO) When closing a Type 5 assessment, the following language must be included in the synopsis section of the closing EC:

- (U//FOUO) For a Type 5 assessment closed on a specific, named individual who is then opened as a CHS _____

  o (U//FOUO) "The information from this assessment must be maintained _____

  o (U//FOUO) (Note: All documentation related to the successfully recruited PCHS must be transferred out of Sentinel and placed into the newly opened CHS's _____ _____

- (U//FOUO) For all other Type 5 assessments, "This assessment did not warrant further investigative effort at this time."

(U//FOUO) Any dissemination from a closed Type 5 assessment must be conducted in accordance with dissemination guidance on CHS closed files and consistent with the principles discussed in Section 15, "Disclosure of a Confidential Human Source's Identity."

3.10.1.   (U) File Maintenance and Disposition

(U//FOUO) Inasmuch as _____ is the official recordkeeping system for FBI CHS records, all   b3 b7E
CHS-related documentation must be serialized _____ unless specified otherwise (see Section 16, "Administration of Confidential Human Sources"). However, until Type 5 assessment files can be managed _____ open and closed legacy paper files or records serialized into Sentinel must be maintained _____ or safeguarded as "prohibited" files in Sentinel. Records relating

to PCHSs that are in the identification, evaluation, and recruitment phases are filed into the [ ] classification or the [ ]

b3
b7E

(U) The disposition of closed Type 5 assessment legacy paper files is as follows:

- (U//~~FOUO~~) Files for Type 5 assessments in the identification phase must be destroyed five years after the files have been closed.

- (U//~~FOUO~~) Files for Type 5 assessments in the evaluation and recruitment phases must be destroyed five years after the files have been closed. The approved disposition authority for records filed under classification [ ] is N1-065-09-27, Item 1a.

b3
b7E

- (U//~~FOUO~~) Once a PCHS has been successfully recruited and his or her records have been imaged, verified as complete and accurate, and placed [ ] under a unique source number, all hardcopy records related to the CHS that have been filed under the [ ] may be destroyed. Records related to a PCHS that are created in Sentinel are not authorized for disposal at this time and must be retained until a disposition schedule is approved for these records.

4. (U) Opening and Reopening a Confidential Human Source

4.1. (U) Use of the Confidential Human Source Program

(U) The AGG-CHS define a CHS as:

> (U) Any individual who is believed to be providing useful and credible information to the FBI for any authorized information collection activity, and from whom the FBI expects or intends to obtain additional useful and credible information in the future, and whose identity, information, or relationship with the FBI warrants confidential handling.

(U//FOUO) Use of the CHS Program should comport with this definition and be based on the following criteria:

- (U) The FBI has established a relationship with an individual who is aware that he or she is working with a representative of the FBI, and the FBI intends for the relationship to be ongoing.

- (U) The FBI receives valuable information from the individual on a recurring basis in support of an FBI assessment or a predicated investigation, whether in response to taskings or as volunteered information.

- (U) The individual's relationship with the FBI creates a need for confidentiality.

(U) An SA must not open an individual as a CHS if there is no logical reason for confidentiality or if the individual holds a position that would normally compel him or her to provide the information. In addition, sworn U.S. LEOs may not be opened as CHSs. The only exception to this rule is that the SAC may approve the operation of a sworn LEO who has agreed to report on matters involving civil rights or public corruption within his or her employing entity. Similarly, crime victims generally should not be opened as CHSs because their use is limited in terms of time and the nature of the assistance they will provide.

4.2. (U) When a Confidential Human Source May Be Tasked

(U//FOUO) A CHS may be tasked to collect information, intelligence, and evidence and/or provide other assistance only when all of the following have been accomplished:

1. (U//FOUO) The opening communication has been approved.
2. (U//FOUO) All requisite approvals, including those from agencies outside the FBI (if necessary), have been obtained.
3. (U//FOUO) The CHS has been provided the appropriate admonishments regarding the nature and parameters of his or her relationship with the FBI (see Section 5, "Confidential Human Source Admonishments").
4. (U//FOUO) Required approvals for the specific tasking (e.g. [   ] or consensual monitoring) have been obtained.   b3 b7E
5. (U//FOUO) The CHS has met with the co-CA.

4.3. (U) Source's Opening Communication

(U//FOUO) Before an SA prepares the source's opening communication, the FO must conduct a universal query to determine whether the individual has already been opened as a CHS in another FO [   ] In addition, the SA must do a deconfliction search [   ]

[   ] to ensure that the individual in question is not currently open in another office or was previously opened as a CHS. This search must be completed and the results noted within the opening communication. FOs are also expected to conduct local queries and more comprehensive searches, as appropriate, and to document the results in the opening communication, as set forth below.

(U//FOUO) If the CHS was previously opened, the new opening communication must state the reason why the CHS was closed. If the CHS was closed for cause, either by the FBI or another agency, additional approvals and review will be required. (See subsection 4.5.1., "Request to Reopen a Confidential Human Source Previously Closed for Cause," and subsection 18.3., "Future Contact with a Closed Confidential Human Source".) If the individual was not previously opened, the communication should simply state that the required deconfliction search was completed with negative results.

(U//FOUO) Only an SA (CA or co-CA) may prepare the source's opening communication. A TFO assigned as a co-CA is not permitted to prepare the opening communication. The SSA must review the communication and determine if the individual may be opened as a CHS. If the SSA approves the communication, notification of the opening must be sent to the appropriate [   ] unit. Other approvals and/or notifications described elsewhere in this PG, such as approvals that must be made by the SAC or by other agencies, may also be required.

(U//FOUO) The [   ] must contain:

   1. (U//FOUO) [   ]
      • (U//FOUO) [   ]

      • (U//FOUO) [   ]
      • (U//FOUO) [   ]
      • (U//FOUO) [   ]

      • (U//FOUO) [   ]
      • (U//FOUO) [   ]
      • (U//FOUO) [   ]
      • (U//FOUO) [   ]

      • (U//FOUO) [   ]
      • (U//FOUO) [   ]
      • (U//FOUO) [   ]

      • (U//FOUO) [   ]
   2. (U//FOUO) [   ]

- (U//FOUO) Whether the person currently has, or previously had, a relationship with any other LE or intelligence agency and, if so, the name of the agency involved. If the person was a CHS who was closed by another agency, reasonable efforts should be made to determine why the CHS was closed, and the SA must document that reason in the opening communication. If the SA ascertains that the person was closed by another agency for a reason that, under FBI policy [ ] additional approvals and review will be required. (See subsection 4.5., "Requirements for Reopening a Confidential Human Source," and subsection 18.3., "Future Contact With a Closed Confidential Human Source.") The SA must describe, in the opening communication, the strategy to be used to mitigate any issues posed by operating the CHS.

  b3
  b7E

  (S//NF) [ ]

  b1
  b3
  b7E

- (U//FOUO) Whether the CHS was previously opened as a CHS by the FBI. If so, state the reason why the CHS was closed. If the CHS was closed for cause, either by the FBI or another agency, additional approvals and review will be required. See subsection 4.5., "Requirements for Reopening a Confidential Human Source," and subsection 18.3., "Future Contact With a Closed Confidential Human Source."

- (U//FOUO) Any promises or benefits that have been given to the CHS by the FBI, the FPO, or any other prosecuting or LE agency (if known after exercising reasonable efforts), and the terms of such promises or benefits.

3. (U//FOUO) Information related to operating the CHS, including:

- (U//FOUO) The investigative classification(s) and/or threat on which the person is expected to provide information and the type of information he or she is expected to provide.

- (U//FOUO) The geographical areas of operation (e.g. [ ] states, cities, and zip codes) where the CHS could be used.

  b3
  b7E

- (U//FOUO) The subject or group on whom the CHS is expected to report.

- (U//FOUO) The CA's and co-CA's names. The SA must state whether the co-CA is an SA or a TFO; if the co-CA is a TFO, the opening communication must identify the TFO's agency and indicate whether that agency brought the CHS to the FBI.

- (U//FOUO) Documentation that the co-CA has met the CHS. If this meeting has not yet occurred when the CHS is opened, it must take place before the CHS is tasked and must be documented in the CHS's [ ] The meeting may be documented by any communication that evidences the co-CA's presence, such as a CHS reporting document, a payment receipt, or admonishments.

- (U//FOUO) The FO and squad [ ] office that will operate the CHS.

  b3
  b7E

- (U//FOUO) [ ]

- (U//FOUO) [ ]

- (U//~~FOUO~~) All likely motivations the CHS could have for providing information,

b3
b7E

- (U//~~FOUO~~)

- (U//~~FOUO~~) Whether approvals are required pursuant to Section 6, "Confidential Human Sources Requiring Department of Justice Approval for Operation." If so, a lead must be sent to the [   ] to notify the Human Source Review Committee (HSRC).

4. (U) Items pertaining to the CHS's background, including:

- (U//~~FOUO~~)

b1
b3
b7E

- ~~(S//NF)~~

- (U)

b3
b7E

- (U//~~FOUO~~) A synopsis of positive search results in

- (U//~~FOUO~~) A synopsis of positive search results of [   ] records checks.

- (U//~~FOUO~~) A synopsis of positive search results of the National Crime Information Center (NCIC)

b3
b7E

- (U//~~FOUO~~) Any relationship the person has with any FBI employee

4.4. (U) Additional Background Information and Records Checks

(U//~~FOUO~~) The information listed below, if reasonable to obtain, must be documented before the CHS is tasked and updated promptly if it changes.

- (U//~~FOUO~~) Past occupations,

b3
b7E

- (U//~~FOUO~~)

- (U//~~FOUO~~)

- (U//~~FOUO~~)

- (U//FOUO) E-mail address [REDACTED]
- (U//FOUO) [REDACTED]
- (U//FOUO) Addresses of past residences
- (U//FOUO) [REDACTED]
- (U//FOUO) [REDACTED]

(U) The records checks listed below must be made if deemed useful in evaluating the individual's background or anticipated operation. They include:

- (S//NF) [REDACTED]
- (U//FOUO) [REDACTED]
- (U//FOUO) [REDACTED]
- (U//FOUO) [REDACTED]

(U//FOUO) [REDACTED]

b3
b7E

b1
b3
b7E

b3
b7E

b3
b7E

(U//FOUO)   b3
b7E

(U//FOUO)   b3
b7E

4.5.   (U) Requirements for Reopening a Confidential Human Source

(U//FOUO) In order to reopen a CHS who was previously closed, the SA must generate a source reopening communication, which must:

- (U//FOUO)   b3
b7E

- (U//FOUO) Satisfy the requirements of subsection 4.3., "Source's Opening Communication."

- (U//FOUO) Indicate that the CHS is being reopened and provide the reason why he or she was previously closed. If the CHS was ever closed for cause during any prior period of operation, then both the reopening procedures and approvals set forth in subsection 4.5.1., "Request to Reopen a Confidential Human Source Previously Closed for Cause," and the provisions in subsection 18.1.2., "Closing a Confidential Human Source for Cause," apply.

(U//FOUO) The approval levels for reopening a CHS are the same as those for opening a CHS for the first time, unless the CHS's status has changed so as to require additional approval (see Section 6, "Confidential Human Sources Requiring Department of Justice Approval for Operation," and Section 7, "Confidential Human Sources Requiring Additional Approvals"), and/or the CHS was closed for cause during any period of operation. If the CHS was previously closed for cause, the approvals set forth in subsection 4.5.1., "Request to Reopen a Confidential Human Source Previously Closed for Cause," apply.

4.5.1.   (U) Request to Reopen a Confidential Human Source Previously Closed for Cause

(U//FOUO) Before initiating contact with, or responding to contact from, a CHS previously closed for cause, SSA approval must be obtained in accordance with subsection 18.3., "Future Contact With a Closed Confidential Human Source."

(U//FOUO) A request to open a CHS previously closed for cause must include the information described in subsection 4.5. After stating that the CHS was closed for cause and the reason why he or she was closed, the following additional information must be provided:

- (U//FOUO) The date on which the CHS was closed for cause or, if the CHS was closed for cause on more than one occasion, the date of each such closure

- (U//FOUO) Details supporting each decision to close the CHS for cause

- (U//FOUO) Details regarding the [ ] if reopening is approved   b3
                                                                          b7E

- (U//FOUO) [ ]
  [ ] the objectives for the case

- (U//FOUO) [ ]

(S//NF) [ ]   b1
                     b3
                     b7E

4.5.2.   (U) Closed Confidential Human Source Reopened by Another Field Office

(U//FOUO) When a closed CHS from one FO is reopened in another FO, the previous FO [ ]   b3
must furnish copies of any documents in the file that are not available [ ] to the new   b7E
FO [ ] Upon request, a copy of the entire file must be sent to the new FO [ ] In addition,
the new office of origin (OO) [ ] must promptly be provided with any information that
reflects negatively upon the reliability of the CHS.

5. (U//~~FOUO~~) Confidential Human Source Admonishments

5.1. (U) Timing and Provision of Admonishments

(U//~~FOUO~~) A CHS must be provided all required and applicable admonishments detailed in this section before the CHS may be tasked and within 90 calendar days after all required approvals have been obtained. After these initial admonishments have been provided to the CHS at opening, they must be provided to the CHS whenever it appears necessary or prudent to do so, and at least once during each 365-day period.

(U//~~FOUO~~) Admonishments must be provided by at least one FBI agent, [ ]   b3
                                                                                                b7E

be retained in the CHS's [ ] file.

(U//~~FOUO~~) The content and meaning of each admonishment must be clearly conveyed to the CHS. Immediately after the admonishments have been given, the SA must require the CHS to acknowledge receipt and understanding of the admonishments. The SA [ ] must document in the CHS's [ ] that they reviewed the admonishments with the CHS and that the CHS acknowledged his or her receipt and understanding of the admonishments. As soon as practicable thereafter, the SSA must review and approve the admonishment documentation.

5.2. (U) Required Admonishments

(U//~~FOUO~~) An SA must provide the following admonishments, which are taken directly from the AGG-CHS, to the CHS. The admonishments need not be read or presented verbatim to the CHS, but must clearly convey that:

- (U//~~FOUO~~) The CHS's assistance and the information provided to the FBI are voluntary.

- (U//~~FOUO~~) The CHS must abide by the admonishments of the FBI and must not take or seek to take any independent actions on behalf of the USG.

- (U//~~FOUO~~) The CHS must provide truthful information to the FBI.

- (U//~~FOUO~~) The USG will strive to protect the CHS's identity, but cannot guarantee that it will not be divulged.

(U//~~FOUO~~) Each time a CHS who is subject to the AGG-CHS receives any rewards, payments, or other compensation from the FBI, the CHS must be advised at the time of payment that he or she is liable for any federal, state, or local taxes that may be owed on that compensation. All CHSs operating domestically (in any U.S. territory) and CHSs operating internationally, but who are reasonably likely to testify in [ ] cases, are subject to the AGG-CHS and must   b3
be provided this instruction.   b7E

5.3. (U) Additional Admonishments

(U//~~FOUO~~) The AGG-CHS require that additional admonishments be provided to the CHS if they are applicable to the particular circumstances of the CHS, or as they become applicable. The

(U) Confidential Human Source Policy Guide

delivering FBI agent [_____] must document in the CHS's [____] file (via the CHS   **b3**
Admonishment form) that the additional admonishments have been provided and that the CHS   **b7E**
acknowledged receipt and understanding of the admonishments.

(U//FOUO) The content and meaning of the following admonishments must be clearly conveyed:

- (U//FOUO) The FBI cannot, on its own, promise or agree to any immunity from prosecution or other consideration by an FPO, a state or local prosecutor, or a court in exchange for the CHS's cooperation, because the decision to confer any such benefit lies within the exclusive discretion of the prosecutor and the court. However, the FBI will consider (but not necessarily act upon) advising the appropriate prosecutor of the nature and extent of the CHS's assistance to the FBI. (This instruction must be given if there is any apparent issue of criminal liability or penalty.)

- (U//FOUO) [_____] the CHS is not authorized to   **b3**
engage in any criminal activity and has no immunity from prosecution for any   **b7E**
unauthorized criminal activity [_____]
[_____] The instruction must be given if the CHS is suspected of committing [_____] See Section 12, "Confidential Human Source
Participation [_____] and Section 13, "Confidential Human
Source Participation [_____]

- (U//FOUO) The CHS is not an employee of the USG and may not represent himself or herself as such, except under circumstances where the CHS has previously been, and continues to be, otherwise employed by the USG.

- (U//FOUO) The CHS may not enter into any contract or incur any obligation on behalf of the USG [_____] or under   **b3**
circumstances where the CHS is otherwise authorized to enter into a contract or incur an   **b7E**
obligation on the behalf of the United States.

- (U//FOUO) [_____]

- (U//FOUO) The FBI cannot guarantee any rewards, payments, or other compensation to [_____]

5.3.1. (U) [_____]   **b3**
(U//FOUO) [_____]   **b7E**

5.3.2. (U) [_____]
(U//FOUO) [_____]

(U) Confidential Human Source Policy Guide

5.3.3. (U)

b3
b7E

(U//~~FOUO~~)

5.3.4. (U)

(U//~~FOUO~~)

6. (U//FOUO) Confidential Human Sources Requiring Department of Justice Approval for Operation

6.1. (U) Types of Confidential Human Sources That Require Department of Justice Approval

(U//FOUO) The CHS opening communication must be completed and approved by an SSA. This triggers the [   ] coordination with DOJ pursuant to subsection 6.2, "Department of Justice Review Procedure for CHSs Requiring Department of Justice Approval." During the DOJ review and approval process, the CHS may be operated in accordance with this PG.

b3
b7

6.1.1. (U) [redacted]

(U//FOUO) [redacted]

[U//FOUO] [redacted]

6.1.2. (U) [redacted]

(U//FOUO) [redacted]

1. (U//FOUO) [redacted]

2. (U//FOUO) [redacted]

b3
b7

6.1.3. (U) [redacted]

(U//FOUO) [redacted]

6.1.4. (U//FOUO) [redacted]

(U//FOUO) [redacted]

(U//FOUO) [redacted]

b3
b7

b3
b7E

6.1.4.1. (U)

(U//FOUO)

6.1.4.2. (U)

(U//FOUO)

6.1.4.3. (U)

b3
b7E

(U//FOUO)

6.1.5. (U)

(U//FOUO)

6.1.6. (U//FOUO)

b3
b7E

(U)

(U//FOUO)

(U//~FOUO~) [   ]   b3
                                                                      b7E

[blank redacted box]

(U//~FOUO~) The SAC may consider the following factors to determine whether "good cause" exists to continue the CA assignment:

- (U//~FOUO~) [   ]   b3
  [   ]   b7E

- (U//~FOUO~) [   ]
  [   ]

- (U//~FOUO~) [   ]
  [   ]

(U//~FOUO~) ASAC approval is required for the assignment [   ]
[   ] This approval may not be delegated.

6.2.   (U) [   ]
[   ]

(U//~FOUO~) DOJ approval is required for the continued operation of any CHS who falls into the categories listed in subsections 6.1.1. through 6.1.5., [   ]   b3
[   ]   b7E
(See AGG-CHS, paragraph I.(B)(2) for the definition of FPO.) DOJ approval is required for all

[blank redacted box]

6.2.1.   (U) [   ]
[   ]

(U//~FOUO~) DOJ, NSD must approve the continued operation of all CHSs requiring DOJ approval who are reporting on national security investigations or foreign intelligence collection, except as provided in subsection 6.2.

(U//~FOUO~) Upon opening, the CA or co-CA must document the CHS's status as a CHS requiring DOJ approval in the source's opening communication and document the status in the FOASR. [   ]   b3
[   ]   b7E

(U//~FOUO~) [   ] approves the continued operation of the CHS, [   ] must provide notice of that approval to the DOJ/NSD within 60 calendar days of the approval. Upon request,

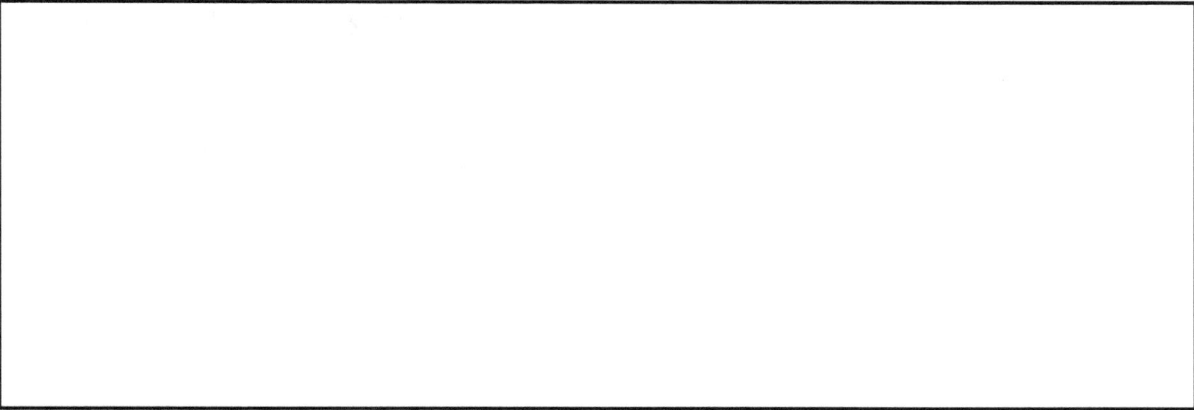

b3
b7E

(U) If a previously opened CHS has a change of status that requires DOJ approval, the CA or co-CA must complete and submit the CHS's status as a CHS requiring DOJ approval on the _____ form and document the CHS's status in the FOASR.

b3
b7E

(U//FOUO) For additional validation guidance on _____

6.2.2. **(U)** _____

(U) The HSRC, which is composed of DOJ and FBI representatives, must approve the continued operation of all CHSs requiring DOJ approval who are not reporting on national security investigations or foreign intelligence collection, except for as provided in subsection 6.2., "Department of Justice Review Procedure for Confidential Human Sources Requiring Department of Justice Approval." Upon opening the CHS, the CA must document the CHS's status as a CHS requiring DOJ approval in the source's opening communication and document this status in the FOASR.

b3
b7E

(U//FOUO) If a previously opened CHS has a change of status that requires DOJ approval, the CA or co-CA must complete and submit the HSRC questionnaire. The CA or co-CA must also document the change of status in the FOASR.

(U//FOUO) The appropriate ____ unit must seek HRSC written approval for the continued operation of a CHS who falls within the definitions in subsections 6.1.1. through 6.1.5. In the case of _____ the appropriate ____ unit must seek written approval for the continued operation of the CHS upon completion of the enhanced review ____ must provide relevant information concerning the use of the CHS to the HSRC, including any annual validation reports. The CHS's identity, however, must not be disclosed unless the FBI chairperson of the HSRC determines that compelling reasons exist to warrant such a disclosure. The HSRC approval process must be completed no later than 45 calendar days after the appropriate ____ unit has submitted the request for continued operation of the CHS. The CHS may continue to be operated during the HSRC review process.

7. (U//~~FOUO~~) Confidential Human Sources Requiring Additional Approvals

(U//~~FOUO~~) The CHSs listed in this section have characteristics that require higher levels of approval.

7.1. (U)   b3
       b7E

(U//~~FOUO~~)

(U//~~FOUO~~)

(U//~~FOUO~~)

7.2. (U)   b3
       b7E

(U//~~FOUO~~) The approvals and procedures addressed in this subsection apply

7.2.1. (U)

(U//~~FOUO~~) The opening communication must document the notification to the FPO attorney assigned to the matter in which the CHS will assist. It must also document the permission obtained by the FO from the appropriate authority   as follows: b3
       b7E

- (U//~~FOUO~~)

- (U//~~FOUO~~)

- (U//~~FOUO~~)

(U//~~FOUO~~)

(U//FOUO) Upon completion of the above, the CA must follow the coordination and approval procedures set forth in DIOG Appendix C. This process involves consultation with the FBIHQ ▢▢▢▢▢▢ b3 b7E

DOJ's Office of Enforcement Operations (OEO).

7.3. (U) ▢▢▢▢▢▢▢▢

(U//FOUO) ▢▢

(U//FOUO) ▢▢▢▢▢▢▢▢▢▢▢▢▢▢▢▢▢▢▢▢▢▢▢▢▢▢▢▢▢▢▢▢▢▢▢▢▢▢▢

(U//FOUO) ▢▢▢▢▢▢▢▢▢▢▢▢▢▢▢▢▢▢▢▢▢▢▢▢▢▢ b3 b7E

(U//FOUO) If an FPO is participating in an investigation using the CHS or will be working with the CHS in connection with a prosecution, the CA must notify the FPO attorney assigned to the matter prior to opening the CHS and must document the notification in the CHS opening communication.

7.3.1. (U) ▢▢▢▢▢▢▢▢

(U//FOUO) ▢▢▢▢▢▢▢▢▢▢▢▢▢▢▢▢▢▢▢▢▢▢▢▢▢▢▢▢▢▢ ▢▢▢▢▢▢ If an FPO is participating in an investigation ▢▢▢▢▢▢▢ the CA must notify the FPO attorney ▢▢▢▢▢▢▢▢▢▢▢▢▢▢▢▢ assigned to the matter prior to using the CHS.

(U//FOUO) The criteria that must be addressed in the request to the SAC include:

1. (U//FOUO) ▢▢▢▢▢▢▢▢▢▢▢▢▢▢ b3 b7E
2. (U//FOUO) ▢▢▢▢▢▢▢▢▢▢▢▢▢▢▢▢▢▢
3. (U//FOUO) ▢▢▢▢▢▢▢▢▢▢▢▢▢▢▢▢
4. (U//FOUO) ▢▢

5. (U//FOUO) _____ b3
b7E

7.4. (U) _____

(U//FOUO) _____

(U//FOUO) _____ b3
b7E

- (U//FOUO) _____
- (U//FOUO) _____
- (U//FOUO) _____

- (U//FOUO) _____ b3
b7E
- (U//FOUO) _____
- (U//FOUO) _____
- (U//FOUO) _____

- (U//FOUO) _____ b3
b7E
- (U//FOUO) _____

7.5. (U) _____

(U//FOUO) _____

7.6. (U) [redacted]   b3
                                                                          b7E

(U//FOUO) [redacted]

• (U//FOUO) [redacted]

• (U//FOUO) [redacted]

(U//FOUO) [redacted]

7.7. (U) [redacted]   b3
                                                                          b7E

(U//FOUO) [redacted]

7.8. (U) [redacted]   b3
                                                                          b7E

(U//FOUO) [redacted]

• (U//FOUO) [redacted]   b3
                                                                          b7E

• (U//FOUO) [redacted]

• (U//FOUO) [redacted]

• (U//FOUO) [redacted]   b3
                                                                          b7E

• (U//FOUO) [redacted]

• (U//FOUO) [redacted]

(U//FOUO) [redacted]

(U//FOUO) [redacted]

7.9. **(U)** [redacted]

(U//FOUO) SAC approval (cannot be delegated) is required [redacted] regardless of the nature of the CHS's reporting. A court order is required before [redacted] if the individual is going to provide information on the employees of, or the patients in, such a program (see Title 42 Code of Federal Regulations § 2.67). If the individual is being opened to obtain information unrelated to his or her employment or to the employees [redacted] a court order is not required. The type of information the CHS will be tasked to obtain, however, must be documented in the CHS's [redacted]

7.10. **(U//FOUO)** [redacted]

(U//FOUO) An SSA may approve the opening [redacted] and subsection 6.2., "Department of Justice Review Procedure for Confidential Human Sources Requiring Department of Justice Approval."

[redacted]

7.11. **(U)** [redacted]

(U//FOUO) [redacted]

- **(U)** [redacted]
- **(U)** [redacted]
- **(U)** [redacted]
- **(U)** [redacted]
- **(U)** [redacted]
- **(U)** [redacted]
- **(U//FOUO)** [redacted]
- **(U//FOUO)** [redacted]

7.12. **(U)** [REDACTED]   b3
[REDACTED]   b7E

(U//FOUO) [REDACTED]

[REDACTED]

(U//FOUO) The degree of coordination required, as set forth below, will depend upon the position of the individual the FBI wishes to open as a CHS and whether the proposed use of the individual [REDACTED]

(U//FOUO) The CDC and/or OGC should be consulted [REDACTED]

[REDACTED]

7.12.1.   (U//FOUO) Definitions

(U) The following definitions apply to this section:

    1. (U//FOUO) [REDACTED]   b3
        [REDACTED]   b7E

    2. (U//FOUO) [REDACTED]

    3. (U//FOUO) [REDACTED]

7.12.2.   (U//FOUO) Concurrence Requirements

(U//FOUO) [REDACTED]   b3
[REDACTED]   b7E

(U//FOUO) [REDACTED]

   • (U//FOUO) [REDACTED]

   • (U//FOUO) [REDACTED]

7.12.3.   (U//FOUO) Concurrence Procedures

(U//FOUO) [REDACTED]   b3
[REDACTED]   b7E

(U) Confidential Human Source Policy Guide

b3
b7E

- (U)
- (U)
- (U)
- (U)
- (U)
- (U)
- (U)
- (U)
- (U)
- (U)

- (U) The CHS's anticipated activities and taskings
- (U) The results of the CHS's completed background investigation
- (U) The FBI POC and his or her phone number
- (U//~~FOUO~~) A statement of whether the CHS's

b3
b7E

(U//~~FOUO~~)

(U//~~FOUO~~)

- (U) The results of FBIHQ indices checks.
- (U)
- (U//~~FOUO~~)

b3
b7E

- (U//~~FOUO~~)

(U//~~FOUO~~) The CA must then upload the results and any related documents to the CHS

(U//~~FOUO~~)

b3
b7E

- (U//FOUO) The results of FBIHQ indices checks.
- (U//FOUO)

(U//FOUO) _____ The CA must then upload the results and any related documents to the CHS's _____

7.12.3.1. (U//FOUO)

(U//FOUO)

_____ must be sent to the requesting SA and must be serialized into the CHS's _____

7.12.3.2. (U//FOUO) Adjudication Procedures

(U//FOUO)

b3
b7E

(U//FOUO) In the event that a resolution cannot be achieved,

(U//FOUO) In the event that the matter is not resolved at the AD level, the matter will be referred within ten working days after impasse

7.13. (U)

(U//FOUO) _____ is an individual for whom:

b3
b7E

1. (U//FOUO)

–OR–

2. (U//FOUO)

–AND–

3. (U//FOUO)

(U//FOUO)

(U//FOUO) An SA may communicate with a former _____ only if either:

1. (U//FOUO) The communication has been approved in advance by the SSA; _____   b3
   _____   b7E

2. (U//FOUO) The communication was not approved in advance, but was initiated _____
   _____

(U//FOUO) An SA who communicates with a _____ CHS in either of these circumstances must promptly report the communication to the SSA _____
_____ The SA must document the following in the CHS's _____ 1) the communication, (2) the circumstances under which the communication was initiated, (3) approvals that were obtained or a statement that no approvals were obtained, and (4) the entities to whom the communication was reported.

7.14. (U) _____   b3
(U//FOUO) _____   b7E

7.15. (U) _____
_____

(U//FOUO) Prior to opening _____
_____ a CHS, the case agent must obtain SAC approval (nondelegable) and must document in the CHS's opening communication (or in an e-mail serialized to the CHS's _____ a detailed justification explaining why this individual requires the protection of the FBI's CHS Program. All admonishments apply _____
_____ if they are opened as CHSs.

(U//FOUO) SSA-approved payments to an individual in one of the aforementioned categories are restricted to reimbursements for expenses incurred in direct support of an investigation and relocation expenses, if justified and necessary. Compensation to these individuals for their services as CHSs, including lump-sum payments, must be approved by the SAC (this approval may not be delegated). The CA must consult with the CDC, who may confer with the section chief (SC) of the Finance Division's (FD) Procurement Section to determine whether _____   b3
_____ should be used. If applicable, an FPO attorney participating in the conduct of the   b7E
investigation must be consulted regarding these payments.

(U//FOUO) _____ in order for that person to continue to contact or operate other CHSs or subsources is not permitted. Generally, _____
_____
_____
_____

7.16. (U) _____
(U//FOUO) _____
_____

7.17. (U) [   ]   b3
                                                                            b7E
(U//FOUO) [   ]

7.18. (U) [   ]   b3
                                                                            b7E
(U//FOUO) [   ]

9. (U) Immigration Matters

9.1. (U//FOUO) [   ]   b3
                                                            b7E

(U//FOUO) The FBI must initiate procedures [   ] of a CHS who is known to be [   ] This section details the requirements for opening and closing CHSs known to be [   ]

[   ]

9.2. (U) Requirements for Opening, Operating, and Closing

(U//FOUO) A CA may open and operate [   ] as a CHS with SSA approval; however,   b3
the CA [   ]   b7E

[   ]

(U//FOUO) [   ]

[   ]

(U//FOUO) If a determination is made to close the CHS, and the CA [   ]   b3
                                                                                         b7E

[   ]

(U//FOUO) The sponsoring CA is responsible for CHSs [   ] The CA must make reasonable efforts to ensure that these CHSs do not violate any U.S. laws [   ]

(U//FOUO) [   ]   b3
                                                                                         b7E

[   ]

9.3. (U) [   ]

(U//FOUO) Prior to initiating any request [   ] the CA must contact the [   ] to determine whether the [   ] and, if so, the best process to employ.

9.3.1. (U) [redacted]

b3
b7E

(U//FOUO) [redacted]

(U//FOUO) [redacted]

(U//FOUO) To initiate [redacted] and determine the type of [redacted] for which the CHS is qualified and the procedures necessary, the CA should review [redacted] for current application procedures and contact the appropriate [redacted] unit with any questions. When determining whether to submit [redacted] request, the CA should be aware that a [redacted]

b3
b7E

(U//FOUO) [redacted] recipient is the responsibility of the sponsoring FO. The CA must take reasonable measures to ensure that the CHS does not violate any U.S. laws [redacted] If the CA reasonably believes that the CHS has engaged [redacted] the CA must notify the appropriate [redacted] to determine what action must be taken. Furthermore, when the CHS's assistance to the FO has been completed, the CA must notify the appropriate [redacted] the CHS. If the CA seeks [redacted] the CHS following his or her assistance, the CA should contact the appropriate [redacted] to determine the circumstances and criteria that permit this to occur. [redacted]

9.3.1.1. (U [redacted]

b3
b7E

(U//FOUO) [redacted]

(U//FOUO) [redacted]

(U//FOUO) [redacted]

b3
b7E

(U//FOUO) The alternative

9.3.1.2. **(U//FOUO) General Considerations**

9.3.1.2.1. (U)

(U//FOUO) For the
purposes of this section,

b3
b7E

(U//FOUO)

The CA must take reasonable steps to ensure that
Furthermore, the agent must immediately

9.3.1.2.2. (U)

(U//FOUO) A CA should consider whether there is an operational need

b3
b7E

9.3.1.2.3. (U)

(U//FOUO)

b3
b7E

(U//FOUO)

9.3.1.2.4. (U)

(U//~~FOUO~~) [redacted]   b3
b7E

9.3.1.2.5.   (U//~~FOUO~~) [redacted]

(U//~~FOUO~~) The CA should coordinate with [redacted] in his or her FO when submitting an application for [redacted] In addition, [redacted] should be made aware of all renewals, extensions, terminations, arrests, and any other significant changes in the status [redacted] [redacted] functions as an important POC between the FO and the [redacted]

9.3.1.3.   (U//~~FOUO~~) [redacted]   b3
b7E

9.3.1.3.1.   (U//~~FOUO~~) **Requests**

(U//~~FOUO~~) To request [redacted] the CA must contact [redacted] for assistance with completing the [redacted] application and to ensure fieldwide compliance with [redacted] FBI policies. If the request does not meet the criteria, [redacted] will return the request to the requesting agent and provide the appropriate guidance. Once the template has been completed correctly, the request will be forwarded to [redacted] for approval. It typically takes four to eight weeks for the [redacted] to receive a decision [redacted]

9.3.1.3.2.   (U//~~FOUO~~) **Approvals**

(U//~~FOUO~~) [redacted]   b3
b7E

(U//~~FOUO~~) [redacted]   b3
b7E

(U//~~FOUO~~) After receiving the [redacted]

b3
b7E

(U//FOUO)

(U//FOUO)

9.3.1.3.3.   (U//FOUO) Extensions

(U//FOUO) If, for operational purposes,

b3
b7E

Requests that are not updated will not be processed. The request should be submitted at least 30 calendar days prior to the expiration date of the

9.3.1.3.4.   (U//FOUO) Agent Responsibilities

1. (U//FOUO) **Change of date of entry**: The CA should ensure that

b3
b7E

2. (U//FOUO) **Change of issuing**   If there is a need to change the issuing   the CA must notify the appropriate   by e-mail and include a justification for the change. In addition, the CA should contact

3. (U//FOUO)

b3
b7E

b3
b7E

(U//FOUO)

4. (U//FOUO)

5. (U//FOUO)

b3
b7E

6. (U//FOUO)   The agent requesting

7. (U//FOUO)

b3
b7E

b3
b7E

8. (U//FOUO) **Violation of the law**:

b3
b7E

must also follow the procedure in Section 12,
"Confidential Human Source Participation in   If the FO
supports continuing

9.3.1.4. (U) [redacted] b3 b7E

(U//FOUO) [redacted]

9.3.2. (U) [redacted] b3 b7E

(U//FOUO) [redacted]

(U//FOUO) [redacted]

[redacted] (For more information or [redacted]

9.3.2.1. (U) **Authority**

(U//FOUO [redacted] is an administrative remedy of the last resort to [redacted] b3 b7E

[redacted] For these reasons, [redacted] should not be requested if another type of administrative remedy, such as [redacted] is available. If [redacted] is granted, however, [redacted] FOs should contact the appropriate [redacted] unit for guidance [redacted] b3 b7E

9.3.2.2. (U) **Request** [redacted]

(U//FOUO) [redacted] policies and procedures for requesting [redacted] depend on several factors, including [redacted] the agent should contact the appropriate [redacted] for the procedures and documents necessary for processing [redacted]

[REDACTED] different forms and procedures, the CA must contact the appropriate [REDACTED] to determine the appropriate paperwork and procedures.

9.3.2.3.   (U) Approval

(U//FOUO) [REDACTED]

(U//FOUO) [REDACTED] In this case, the agent must provide a copy of the approval to the appropriate [REDACTED] and must serialize the notice to the CHS's [REDACTED]

9.3.2.4.   (U) Extension

(U//FOUO) [REDACTED] the CA must request an extension no later than 30 calendar days before the expiration date. Similar to the initial request, the procedure for an extension varies between [REDACTED] The CA must coordinate with the appropriate [REDACTED] for the appropriate forms and procedures.

9.3.2.5.   (U) [REDACTED]

9.3.2.5.1.   (U//FOUO) Reporting

(U//FOUO) There is no [REDACTED] however, the CA is still required to immediately notify the appropriate [REDACTED] if:

- (U//FOUO) [REDACTED] If the FO wishes to continue [REDACTED] the CA must make the request in an LHM that documents the circumstances [REDACTED] must notify the [REDACTED] FO of [REDACTED] provide the supporting documentation and the request to continue [REDACTED]

- (U//FOUO) [REDACTED] cooperation is no longer needed.

- (U//FOUO) [REDACTED] has otherwise ended his or her cooperation [REDACTED]

- (U//FOUO) The CA [REDACTED] has changed.

9.3.2.5.2.   (U//FOUO) [REDACTED]

(U//FOUO) When [REDACTED] is terminated or has expired, it is the CA's responsibility to exercise due diligence and ensure [REDACTED] the CA must notify the appropriate [REDACTED] the CA must coordinate with the [REDACTED] The CA must note the name and contact information of [REDACTED] In the event that the agent has exercised due diligence but cannot ensure [REDACTED] the agent must notify the appropriate [REDACTED] will, in turn, notify [REDACTED] of the change in status. To complete

b3
b7E

b3
b7E

b3
b7E

b3
b7E

the required reporting in these circumstances, the CA must complete [   ]   b3
[   ] memo, which the [   ] will provide to the agent.   b7E

9.3.3. (U//FOUO) [   ]

(U//FOUO) The CA may request [   ]

[   ] The CA should contact the appropriate [   ] for

[   ]

(U//FOUO) If the CA seeks to obtain [   ] for the CHS following the CHS's assistance to the government, the SA may do so in certain circumstances [   ]

[   ]

9.3.4. (U) [   ]

9.3.4.1. (U) Nature and Purpose of the Program

(U//FOUO) [   ]   b3
b7E

(U//FOUO) [   ]

(U//FOUO) [   ]   b3
b7E

(U//FOUO) [   ]

b3
b7E

9.3.4.1.1. **(U)** ⬚⬚⬚⬚ **Confidential Human Source Involvement** ⬚⬚⬚⬚

(U//FOUO) Once ⬚⬚⬚ has been issued, if the CA reasonably believes the CHS ⬚⬚⬚ ⬚⬚⬚ the CA must notify ⬚⬚⬚⬚⬚⬚⬚⬚⬚ to determine what action must be taken. See Section 12, "Confidential Human Source Participation ⬚⬚⬚ ⬚⬚⬚

b3
b7E

9.3.4.2. **(U)** ⬚⬚⬚⬚⬚

(U//FOUO) ⬚⬚⬚⬚⬚⬚⬚⬚⬚⬚⬚⬚⬚⬚⬚⬚⬚⬚⬚⬚⬚⬚⬚

1. (U//FOUO) ⬚⬚⬚⬚⬚
2. (U//FOUO) ⬚⬚⬚⬚⬚
3. (U//FOUO) ⬚⬚⬚⬚⬚⬚⬚⬚⬚⬚⬚⬚⬚⬚⬚⬚⬚⬚⬚⬚⬚⬚

b3
b7E

4. (U//FOUO) ⬚⬚⬚⬚⬚
5. (U//FOUO) ⬚⬚⬚⬚⬚
6. (U//FOUO) ⬚⬚⬚⬚⬚
7. (U//FOUO) ⬚⬚⬚⬚⬚
8. (U//FOUO) ⬚⬚⬚⬚⬚⬚⬚⬚⬚⬚⬚⬚⬚⬚⬚⬚⬚⬚⬚⬚

b3
b7E

9. (U//FOUO) ⬚⬚⬚⬚⬚
10. (U//FOUO) ⬚⬚⬚⬚⬚⬚⬚⬚⬚⬚⬚⬚⬚

11. (U//FOUO)

12. (U//FOUO)

13. (U//FOUO)

14. (U//FOUO)

15. (U//FOUO)

16. (U//FOUO)

9.3.4.2.1.   (U)

(U//FOUO)

9.3.4.2.2.   (U)

(U//FOUO) Upon the initial submission of the [   ] application to the DOJ, the CA may request [   ] through the appropriate [   ] The CHS must pay the costs [   ] The FBI may not pay for or reimburse the fees as a CHS expense. In addition, the FBI cannot pay or reimburse the CHS for personal living expenses

9.3.5.   (U[   ]

/S//

b1
b3
b7E

9.4. **(U)**

b1
b3
b7E

(S//~~NF~~)

b3
b7E

9.5. **(U//~~FOUO~~)**

(U//~~FOUO~~)  are effective tools for LE and intelligence operations and may be requested for the CHS

(U//~~FOUO~~) the CA must submit to the appropriate ____ unit an LHM detailing a summary of the investigation; a justification for the requested benefit and/or document;  the CHS's identifying information (i.e., name, alien number, sex, DOB, and country of birth).

(U//FOUO) After completion and review of the documents, the ☐ will coordinate with, and forward the appropriate documentation to ☐

b3
b7E

(U//FOUO) ☐

10. (U//~~FOUO~~) Operation of Confidential Human Sources

10.1. (U//~~FOUO~~) Confidential Human Sources Who May Testify in a Court or Other Proceeding

(U//~~FOUO~~) The CA or co-CA must serialize to the CHS's file any documents relating to FPO approvals, notifications, or coordination required in this PG for CHS operational activities (e.g., payments[   ] that may become an issue in court if it becomes necessary for the CHS to testify. **b3** **b7E**

(U//~~FOUO~~) Whenever it becomes apparent that a CHS may have to testify in a court or other proceeding in which he or she is providing assistance to the FBI, the SA must advise the CHS and document the advisement[   ]

(U//~~FOUO~~) The CA or co-CA should be aware that the manner in which a CHS is tasked may subject the CHS to having to testify, even if the CHS's testimony is not anticipated or desired. For instance, if the CHS is tasked[   ] the CHS may later be required to testify. Accordingly, the CA or co-CA must inform the CHS of this prior to tasking the individual in this manner.

(U//~~FOUO~~) Unanticipated situations may also arise that require a CHS to testify, even though the CHS has not previously agreed to do so. For example, if a CHS[   ] it may be necessary for the CHS to testify. If there is a possibility that a court will require[   ] **b3** **b7E**

10.2. (U) Electronic Communications With a Confidential Human Source

(U//~~FOUO~~)[   ] Depending upon the circumstances, in order to protect the CHS and the operation, consideration must be given to the type of investigation the CHS is supporting, the specific interactions required with the CHS, the technical proficiency of the CHS, and whether technical equipment needs to be supplied to the CHS. Overt FBI purchase of equipment supplied to the CHS and the use of overt FBI equipment to communicate with the CHS are not recommended, except in very limited circumstances. Issues related to communications are complex, and possible solutions to hurdles encountered can be discussed with the PM for the Operational Technology Division's (OTD)[   ] The use of solutions proposed by OTD must be documented in the CHS's[   ] **b3** **b7E**

(U//~~FOUO~~) The above-listed electronic communication tools or devices[   ] consequently, the SA must exercise caution in using them. In-person contact is the preferred method of interaction with the CHS. If any of the above methods is used, its use must be documented in the CHS's[   ] In addition, agents should be aware that all communications with a testifying CHS will likely be produced in discovery; therefore, agents must ensure that all communications are essential to operations and professional in content. **b3** **b7E**

(U//FOUO) SSA approval is required for all interaction with a CHS [redacted] b3 b7E
electronic communications, including, but not limited to, e-mails, texts, faxes, [redacted]
[redacted] This approval must be properly
documented in the CHS's file. These communication methods may only be used when
operationally necessary, and proper consideration must be given to operational security,
[redacted] and other means. Additional guidance on proper
operational security can be provided by OTD's [redacted]

(U//FOUO) Use of the above electronic communication methods—as well as telephonic
contact—with a CHS [redacted]
[redacted]

(U//FOUO) Additional guidance on secure communications with a CHS can be provided by b3 b7E
FBIHQ operational divisions and the PM for OTD's [redacted]

10.3. (U) [redacted]

(U//FOUO) [redacted] must comply with the AGG-Dom and DIOG
subsection 18.6.1.

10.4. (U) [redacted]

(U//FOUO) [redacted]

10.5. (U//FOUO) [redacted] b3 b7E

(U//FOUO) [redacted] by CHSs must comply with the AGG-Dom and DIOG Section 16.

10.6. (U//FOUO) [redacted]

(U//FOUO) The FBI's issuance of [redacted] to CHSs is only allowed in extraordinary
circumstances. One of the few areas where [redacted] CHSs have been granted is [redacted]
[redacted]
[redacted] may not be issued to a CHS for the
purpose of providing security following his or her cooperation. The CA or co-CA must use other
methods to provide protection. [redacted]
[redacted]

(U//FOUO) A request [redacted] for a CHS must contain compelling justification, including a b3 b7E
description of the proposed operation of the CHS, and must specify whether the CHS will
operate [redacted] on a full-time or part-time basis. In the FO, the request must be approved
by the [redacted] and the SAC. The request must then be sent to the [redacted]

which will coordinate the approval of the request by the operational unit, the FBIHQ [____] b3 b7E

[____] will advise the FO of the final decision. Documentation related to the request and outcome must be serialized into the CHS's file.

(U//FOUO) If a CHS is issued [____] the FO is responsible for ensuring that it is used in compliance with [____] Under all circumstances, however, the [____] must only be made available to the CHS during operational events and retrieved by the FBI after each operational use. [____]

10.7. (U) Obtaining Information About a [____]   b3 b7E

(U//FOUO) If a [____] who is facing pending criminal charges for which the defendant's Sixth Amendment right to counsel has attached, the [____] regarding the pending charges. A subject's Sixth Amendment right attaches when a prosecution has commenced (i.e., at, or after the initiation of, adversarial judicial criminal proceedings—whether by way of a formal charge, a preliminary hearing, an indictment, a criminal information document, or an arraignment).

(U//FOUO) Nevertheless, a CHS may be directed to [____]

(U//FOUO) In certain circumstances [____] but against whom charges are not pending, may be limited by other laws. (See the Citizen's Protection Act, codified at 28 U.S.C. § 530B.) On any occasion when [____] it is recommended that the CA consult with the FO's CDC.

(U//FOUO) Finally, the CA must instruct the CHS not to interfere with the defendant's attorney-client relationship. For example, [____]   b3 b7E

(U//FOUO) Any questions about the content of this subsection should be directed to the assigned AUSA or to the FO CDC.

10.8. (U//FOUO) Use of a Confidential Human Source Associated With [____]   b3 b7E

(U//FOUO) Before operating a CHS [____]   b3 b7E

[____] the CA or co-CA must consult with the CDC to ensure that the use of the CHS's does not infringe upon the First Amendment right to free speech.

(U//FOUO) The Electronic Communications Privacy Act (ECPA) establishes limitations on the government's access to records and content held by wire or electronic communications service providers, including telephone companies and companies offering communication facilities

through the Internet. Thus, those restrictions [   ] b3
[   ] b7E
[   ] Furthermore, the Fourth Amendment protects
service provider customers from the disclosure of the contents of their communications to the
government.

(U//FOUO) As a general rule, therefore, [   ]
[   ]
[   ] does not constitute compliance with ECPA or the Fourth Amendment.
The CA or co-CA may only obtain such information through applicable legal processes [   ]
[   ]

(U//FOUO) The CDC should be consulted if there are any questions about what information may
be obtained from such a CHS in compliance with ECPA.

10.9. (U) [   ] b3
b7E

(U//FOUO) The FBI may accept information concerning alleged violations of law or other
matters within FBI jurisdiction from [   ] The FBI may not recruit or operate
CHSs for the sole purpose of collecting information concerning the political beliefs or personal
lives of individuals [   ]
[   ] may not knowingly influence or attempt to influence any action
of [   ] unless it is done in furtherance of a compelling governmental interest. If an
investigation plans any activity that may [   ] the SSA, the CA, or the co-CA
must consult with the CDC. In addition, this type of activity may trigger review and approval
requirements for UDP and must comply with the AGG-Dom and with DIOG Section 16.

10.10. (U//FOUO) [   ] b3
b7E

(U//FOUO) [   ]

10.11. (U//FOUO) [   ] b3
b7E

(U//FOUO) [   ]

(U//FOUO) One major exception to this rule is that a CHS may provide [   ]
because this information is not protected and may be voluntarily produced under certain
circumstances. Furthermore, records [   ] are also subject to voluntary production.
The CDC should be consulted if there are any questions about what information may be obtained
from such a CHS [   ]

10.12. (U//FOUO) [redacted]   b3
                                                                                b7E
(U//FOUO) [redacted]

[redacted]

- (U//FOUO) [redacted]

- (U//FOUO) [redacted]

- (U//FOUO) [redacted]

(U//FOUO) [redacted]   b3
                                                                                b7E

[redacted]

10.13. (U//FOUO) [redacted]

(U//FOUO) [redacted]

[redacted]

- (U//FOUO) Whether or not the CHS was paid. SAs may use general terms so that no exact amounts are given, for example, "The CHS was paid a modest fee for information."
- (U//FOUO) [redacted]   b3
                                                                                b7E
- (U//FOUO) [redacted]

10.14. (U//FOUO) [redacted]

(U//FOUO) [redacted]

[redacted]

11. (U) Department of Justice Notification Requirements

(U//FOUO) This section describes situations involving a CHS that require the FBI to notify certain components of the DOJ, in accordance with the AGG-CHS. The DAG must approve exceptions to these notification requirements, as set forth in subsection 11.8, "Exceptions to Department of Justice Notification Requirements." All notifications discussed in subsections 11.3 through 11.5 must be made in writing and approved by the SSA.

11.1. (U) Notification Designees

(U//FOUO) An SAC and a CFP may designate (if both concur) particular individuals in their respective offices to carry out the functions assigned to them in subsections 11.2 ("Notification to the Department of Justice of Unauthorized Illegal Activity") through 11.7 ("Responding to Requests from Federal Prosecuting Office Attorneys Regarding a Confidential Human Source") and subsection 11.9 ("Department of Justice Review of FBI Confidential Human Source Files for Nontestimonial Confidential Human Sources").

11.2. (U) Notification to the Department of Justice of Unauthorized Illegal Activity

(U//FOUO) For notification procedures related to CHS UIA, see Section 12, "Confidential Human Source Participation in Unauthorized Illegal Activity."

11.3. (U) Notification to the Department of Justice of the Investigation or Prosecution of a Confidential Human Source

(U//FOUO) If an SA has reasonable grounds to believe that the alleged felonious activity of a current or former CHS is, or is expected to become, the basis of a prosecution or an investigation by an FPO, the SA must immediately notify a DOJ⬜⬜ or the assigned FPO attorney of that individual's status as a current or former CHS. With respect to a former CHS whose alleged felonious activity is, or is expected to become, the basis of a prosecution or investigation by a state or local prosecutor's office, the DOJ⬜⬜ or assigned FPO attorney must be immediately notified, but only if the SA has reasonable grounds to believe that the CHS's prior relationship with the FBI is material to the prosecution or investigation.   b3 b7E

(U//FOUO) Whenever such a notification occurs, the DOJ's⬜⬜ or the assigned FPO attorney is responsible for notifying the CFP. The CFP and FBI SAC (or designees), with each other's concurrence, must notify any other federal, state, or local prosecutor's office or LE agency that is participating in the investigation or prosecution of the CHS. The notification to other prosecutors or LE agencies must be documented in the CHS's⬜⬜   b3 b7E

(U//FOUO) The SA's notification to the DOJ⬜⬜ or FPO attorney must be made in writing, approved by the SSA, and maintained in the CHS's V⬜⬜

11.4. (U) Notification to the Department of Justice Regarding Certain Federal Judicial Proceedings

(U//FOUO) An SA must immediately notify the appropriate DOJ⬜⬜ or the assigned FPO attorney whenever the agent has reasonable grounds to believe that: b3 b7E

- (U//FOUO) A current or former CHS has been called to testify by the prosecution in any federal grand jury or judicial proceeding.

- (U//FOUO) The statements of a current or former CHS have been, or will be, utilized by the prosecution in any federal judicial proceeding.
- (U//FOUO) An FPO attorney intends to represent to a court or jury that a current or former CHS is or was a coconspirator or other criminally culpable participant in any criminal activity.

(U//FOUO) The notification must be made in writing, approved by the SSA, and maintained in the CHS's V[   ]

11.5. (U) Notification to the Department of Justice of Privileged or Exculpatory Information

(U//FOUO) If an FPO is participating in the conduct of an FBI investigation that is utilizing a CHS or working with a CHS in connection with a prosecution, the CA or co-CA must notify the FPO attorney assigned to the matter—in advance, whenever possible—if the CA or co-CA has reasonable grounds to believe that the CHS will obtain or provide information that is subject to, or arguably subject to, a legal privilege of confidentiality belonging to someone other than the CHS. Documentation that the notification has been made by the CA or co-CA must be serialized in the[   ]

(U//FOUO) Whenever an SA knows or reasonably believes that a current or former CHS has information that is exculpatory as to a target of, or a defendant (including a convicted defendant) in, a federal, state, or local investigation or case, the FBI agent must disclose the exculpatory information to either the assigned FPO attorney who is participating (or who has participated) in the conduct of that investigation or to the DOJ[   ]This disclosure notification must be made in writing, approved by the SSA, and maintained in the CHS's V[   ]

(U//FOUO) In turn, the assigned FPO attorney or the DOJ[   ]is responsible for disclosing the exculpatory information to all affected federal, state, and local authorities. In the event that the disclosure would jeopardize the security of the CHS or seriously compromise an investigation, the FPO attorney or DOJ[   ]must refer the matter to the HSRC for consideration, except for matters related to an[   ] investigation. The latter must be referred to the AAG of the NSD (or designee). The basis for referring the matter to the HSRC or the AAG of NSD (or designee) must be documented in the referral and placed into the CHS's[   ]

11.6. (U//FOUO) [   ]

(U//FOUO) An SA must not name a CHS[   ]unless the SA believes that:

- (U//FOUO)[   ]would endanger the CHS's life or otherwise jeopardize an ongoing investigation.
- (U//FOUO)[   ] based on the CHS's suspected involvement in[   ] See subsection 11.2., "Notification to Department of Justice of Unauthorized Illegal Activity."

(U//~~FOUO~~) If [_____] the SA must inform both the FPO   b3
attorney making the application and the court to which the application is made[_____]   b7E
[_____] The SA notification to the FPO attorney must be made in writing, approved by the
SSA, and documented in the CHS's[_____]

11.7. (U//~~FOUO~~) Responding to Requests From Federal Prosecuting Office Attorneys Regarding Confidential Human Sources

(U//~~FOUO~~) For criminal matters arising under or related to the AGG-CHS, upon request by an
appropriate FPO attorney, the CA or co-CA, in coordination with[_____]must promptly   b3
provide to the FPO attorney all relevant information concerning a CHS, including whether the   b7E
individual is a current or former CHS for the FBI. The dissemination of the relevant information
to the FPO must be approved by the SSA and documented to the CHS's[_____]

(U//~~FOUO~~) If the SAC has an objection to providing this information based on the specific
circumstances of the case, he or she must explain the objection to the FPO attorney making the
request, and any remaining disagreement as to whether the information should be provided to the
FPO attorney must be resolved pursuant to subsection 1.5.1., "AGG-CHS and AGG-Dom
Exceptions and Dispute Resolution."

11.8. (U) Exceptions to Department of Justice Notification Requirements

(U//~~FOUO~~) The Director of the FBI, with the written concurrence of the DAG, may withhold
any notification required pursuant to subsection 11.2., "Notification to the Department of Justice
of Unauthorized Illegal Activity," through subsection 11.7., "Responding to Requests From
Federal Prosecuting Office Attorneys Regarding Confidential Human Sources," if the SAC and
DAG determine that the identity, position, or information provided by the CHS warrants
extraordinary protection for sensitive national security reasons. Any SAC determination to
withhold notification, along with the concurrence of the DAG, must be documented by the CA or
co-CA and maintained in the CHS's[_____]

11.9. (U//~~FOUO~~) Department of Justice Review of Confidential Human Source Files for Nontestimonial Confidential Human Sources

(U//~~FOUO~~) If an FPO attorney seeks to review the file of a CHS who is not expected to testify,
the CA or co-CA must advise the FPO attorney to submit a written request to the FO CDC. The
FPO attorney's request must specify the information sought and provide justification for the
review. After consulting with the CDC and ASAC, the SAC must issue a written response to the
FPO attorney outlining the parameters of any permitted review. The SAC response and the FPO
attorney request must be documented to the CHS's[_____]

(U//~~FOUO~~) If the SAC and FPO agree on the terms of the review, the[_____]must make
arrangements for the CHS file review in FBI office space. The FPO attorney is not permitted to
remove copies of CHS file material from FBI space without CDC approval. The CA or co-CA
must document this agreement in the administrative portion of the CHS's[_____]   b3
                                                                                              b7E

(U//~~FOUO~~) The CA or co-CA must prepare a record of the FPO attorney's CHS file review,
which must include the FPO attorney's request and the SAC's response; the date of the CHS file
review; the identity of the FPO reviewer; the method of review; the identification of any
documents reviewed and, if applicable, of any copies of CHS file material removed from the FBI
office by the FPO reviewer, as well as the written approval of the CDC permitting the document
removal.

(U/~~FOUO~~) The resolution of any disagreement between the FPO attorney and the CDC regarding the printing and release of documents from the CHS's file must be completed in accordance with subsection 1.5.1., "AGG-CHS and AGG-Dom Exceptions and Dispute Resolution."

(U/~~FOUO~~) See also the DAG memorandum titled "Guidance on the Federal Bureau of Investigation's (FBI) Administration of Confidential Human Sources and Its Impact on the Discovery Obligations of Prosecutors" (January 15, 2009).

12. (U) Confidential Human Source [   ]   b3
[   ]   b7E

12.1. (U) Notification Process

(U//FOUO) According to the AGG-CHS, if an FBI agent has reasonable grounds to believe that
a CHS has [   ] the CHS must be closed, unless   b3
SAC approval for continued use is obtained (see subsection 12.2.). The SA must promptly notify   b7E
DOJ's [   ] or the assigned FPO attorney of [   ] and the reasonable grounds upon which
the FBI believes it has occurred. Reasonable grounds exist, for example, when an SA has
(1) knowledge of a pending state or federal investigation of the CHS; (2) knowledge of pending
criminal charges against the CHS; (3) an admission from the CHS; or (4) information from two
or more independent sources, or from one credible source, that the CHS has engaged in illegal
activity. The SA must make the notification even if the CHS will be closed as a result of the
illegal activity. The notification to DOJ must be made in writing, approved by the SSA, and
documented [   ]

(U//FOUO) If the CHS's continued use is desired, approval must be obtained in accordance with
subsection 12.2.

(U//FOUO) After being notified by the FBI, the DOJ's [   ] or assigned FPO attorney is   b3
responsible for notifying the following FPOs of the CHS's criminal activity and the individual's   b7E
status as a CHS:

- (U//FOUO) The FPO in whose district the criminal activity primarily occurred, unless a
  state or a local prosecuting office in that district has filed charges against the CHS for the
  criminal activity, and there is no basis for federal prosecution in that district

- (U//FOUO) The FPO attorney, if any, who is participating in the conduct of an
  investigation that is utilizing the CHS or is working with the CHS in connection with a
  prosecution

- (U//FOUO) [   ]

(U//FOUO) Whenever these notifications are provided, the CFP and the SAC (or the individual
to whom authority has been delegated in accordance with subsection 11.1., "Notification
Designees"), with the other's concurrence, must notify any state or local prosecutor's office that
has jurisdiction over the CHS's criminal activity and that has not already filed charges against
the CHS for the criminal activity, that the CHS has engaged in criminal activity. If the state and
local prosecutor's office is known to already be aware of the CHS's criminal activity, then
notification by the CFP and SAC is unnecessary. The CFP(s) and the SAC(s) are not required to
notify the state and local prosecutor's office of the person's status as a CHS, but may do so with
each other's concurrence. These notifications must be documented in the CHS's [   ]   b3
b7E

12.2. (U//FOUO) Request for Approval of the Continued Operation of a Confidential Human Source

(U//FOUO) When a CA has reasonable grounds to believe that a CHS has engaged in UIA, but
wishes to continue to use the CHS, the CA must submit a request for continued operation to the
SAC (nondelegable) for approval in addition to reporting the UIA to DOJ in accordance with
subsection 12.1., "Notification Process" [   ]

(U//FOUO) The request must address:

- (U//FOUO)   b3
                                                                               b7E
- (U//FOUO)

- (U//FOUO)
- (U//FOUO)
- (U//FOUO)
- (U//FOUO)

(U//FOUO) If the SAC approves the continued use of the CHS, the CA must re-admonish the   b3
CHS with regard to participation[   ]and remind the CHS that he or she has no immunity   b7E
from prosecution for the unauthorized activity. The CA must document the request to continue
CHS use and the outcome of the request in the CHS's[   ]

12.3. (U//FOUO[   ]

(U//FOUO) When a CA has reason to believe that a CHS[   ]   b3
                                                                                               b7E

13. (U//~~FOUO~~) Confidential Human Source [   ]

b3
b7E

(U//~~FOUO~~) Under certain circumstances described in this section, [   ]

13.1. (U) [   ]

(U//~~FOUO~~) According to the AGG-CHS, [   ]

- (U//~~FOUO~~) [   ]

- (U//~~FOUO~~) [   ]

b3
b7E

(U//~~FOUO~~) [   ]

13.2. (U) [   ]

13.2.1. (U) [   ] Definition[4]

(U//~~FOUO~~) The AGG-CHS defines [   ]

b3
b7E

1. (U//~~FOUO~~) [   ]

2. (U//~~FOUO~~) [   ]

---

[3] (U) Per the AGG-Dom [   ]

b3
b7E

[4] (U//~~FOUO~~) While the AGG-CHS definition [   ] generally does not include [   ]

[5] (U) [   ]

3. (U//~~FOUO~~) [redacted]   b3
                                                                                b7E

4. (U//~~FOUO~~) [redacted]

5. (U//~~FOUO~~) [redacted]

6. (U//~~FOUO~~) [redacted]

13.2.2.   (U) [redacted] **Authorization**

(U//~~FOUO~~) [redacted] requires advance written approval by the FO SAC. [redacted]   b3
[redacted] must contain the authorization in accordance with subsection 13.9., "Recordkeeping   b7E
Procedures."

(U//~~FOUO~~) In criminal investigations, the SA must contact (following the SAC's approval[7]) the
FPO involved in the investigation to obtain the appropriate CFP authorization in writing. The
AGG-CHS allow the SAC and CFP to agree to designate particular individuals at the supervisory
level (i.e., ASAC) in their respective offices to carry out the approval functions assigned to them.

(U//~~FOUO~~) The appropriate CFP for all investigations, except national security investigations, is
the CFP who:

- (U//~~FOUO~~) Is participating in an FBI investigation that is utilizing the CHS or working
  with that CHS in connection with a prosecution.

- (U//~~FOUO~~) Would have primary jurisdiction [redacted]

                                    –OR–

- (U//~~FOUO~~) Is located where [redacted]   b3
                                                                                b7E

(U//~~FOUO~~) For national security investigations or foreign intelligence collection, the CA must
send, upon SAC approval, an EC to the appropriate FBIHQ operational unit to obtain AD
[redacted] thereafter, the FBIHQ operational unit must forward the AD-approved

[6] (U) [redacted] Any ambiguities in
this regard must be resolved by the AAG for the Criminal Division.

[7] (U//~~FOUO~~) While the AGG-CHS only require SAC approval internally, current FBI practice for national security
matters is to obtain FBIHQ operational AD approval after the SAC [redacted] and then forward the
approved request to the appropriate DOJ authority for its approval. The FO is not responsible for seeking DOJ
approval in national security or foreign intelligence collection matters.

request, in a document suitable for dissemination, to the appropriate DOJ authority for its approval. The FBIHQ operational unit must then notify the requesting FO, via EC, upon DOJ approval or denial of the request. A copy of the above [ ] documentation must be serialized to [ ]

b3
b7E

(U//FOUO) The appropriate CFP for national security and foreign intelligence collection matters is the AAG of the DOJ NSD or his or her designee. This designee may be an FPO attorney; however, [ ] must verify that the delegation has taken place within the relevant FPO. If [ ] is unable to identify an NSD designee, the FO should request assistance from the operational unit at FBIHQ.

(U//FOUO) As part of the approval process, the SAC and CFP [ ] must make specific findings, as set forth in subsection 13.4., "Documented Findings of [ ] Approvers," [ ] which must be documented in the response [ ] This documentation must be maintained [ ]

13.2.2.1.   (U//FOUO) CFP Authorization [ ]

b3
b7E

(U//FOUO) For guidance on this authorization see DIOG subsection 17.6. [ ]

13.2.3.   (U//FOUO) [ ] **Emergency Oral Authorization**

(U//FOUO) Those authorized to approve [ ] in accordance with subsection 13.2.2., [ ] Authorization," may orally authorize a CHS [ ] without advance written documentation when they each determine that:

- (U//FOUO) A highly significant and unanticipated investigative opportunity would be lost if the [ ] written authorization procedures were followed.
- (U//FOUO) These circumstances would support a finding to authorize [ ] pursuant to subsection 13.4., "Documented Findings of [ ] Approvers."

b3
b7E

(U//FOUO) In such an event, the documentation requirements, including a written justification for the oral authorization, must be completed as soon as practicable, but within 72 hours following the oral approval [ ]

13.2.4.   (U) [ ] **Duration**

(U//FOUO) [ ] authorization must be set for a specified period [ ] days. An exception exists for national security investigations or foreign intelligence collection, for which the CFP may authorize [ ]

(U//FOUO) The [ ] authorization period may be extended, according to the procedures set forth in subsection 13.6., "Renewal and Expansion [ ]

b3
b7E

13.3.   (U) [ ]

(U//FOUO) According to the AGG-CHS, [ ] is any other activity that would constitute a [ ]

13.3.1. (U)[   ]**Authorization**   b3
    b7E

(U//~~FOUO~~)[   ]requires the advance written approval (absent a request for emergency authorization in accordance with subsection 13.3.4 ,[   ] Duration") of the SAC. The authorization communication must contain specific findings regarding the proposed[   ]as set forth in subsection 13.4 , "Documented Findings of [   ]Approvers," and must be maintained[   ]

13.3.2. (U) **Coordination With the Federal Prosecuting Office Attorney**

(U//~~FOUO~~) FPO approval is not required for[   ]however, if an FPO attorney is assigned to an investigation in which the CHS is assisting and the CHS is expected to testify, the CA must ensure that the FPO attorney is notified in advance[   ]if practicable[   ] request must document the FO's written or oral notification in the[   ]

13.3.3. (U)[   ]**Emergency Oral Authorization**   b3
    b7E

(U//~~FOUO~~) In extraordinary circumstances, an SAC may orally authorize a CHS[   ] [   ]without advance documentation, after determining that a highly significant and unanticipated investigative opportunity would be lost if the FO were to follow the[ ]written authorization procedures. In such an event, the SAC must complete the documentation requirements, including as written justification for the oral authorization, as soon as practicable, [   ]must document this approval communication.

13.3.4. (U)[   ]**Duration**

(U//~~FOUO~~)[   ]authorization must be set for a specified period[   ] [   ]

(U//~~FOUO~~)[   ]authorization period may be extended, according to the procedures set forth in subsection 13.6., "Renewal and Expansion of[   ] [   ]

13.4. (U)[   ]   b3
    b7E

(U//~~FOUO~~)[   ]

[   ]

1. (U//~~FOUO~~)[   ]

[   ]

−OR−

2. (U//~~FOUO~~)[   ]   b3
    b7E

(U//~~FOUO~~)[   ]

- (U//~~FOUO~~)[   ]
- (U//~~FOUO~~)[   ]
- (U//~~FOUO~~)[   ]

[   ]

- (U//FOUO) _____ b3 b7E
- (U//FOUO) _____

  _____
- (U//FOUO) _____
  _____
- (U//FOUO) _____
  _____

13.4.1. (U) Precautionary Measures

(U//FOUO) Whenever an SA has obtained authorization for a CHS to [_____] the SA b3 b7E
must take all reasonable steps to:

- (U//FOUO) _____
- (U//FOUO) _____
- (U//FOUO) _____
  _____

13.5. (U) Admonishments Related to [_____]

(U//FOUO) If a CHS [_____], two SAs—or one SA [_____]
[_____]—must review written admonishments with the CHS that state, at a
minimum, that:

- (U//FOUO) _____ b3 b7E
  _____
- (U//FOUO) _____
  authorization.
- (U//FOUO) The CHS may not, under any circumstances:
  - (U//FOUO) Participate in an act of violence [_____]
  - (U//FOUO) _____ b3 b7E
    _____
  - (U//FOUO) _____
    _____
  - (U//FOUO) _____
    _____
- (U//FOUO) _____
  _____

- (U//FOUO) _____   b3
  _____   b7E

(U//FOUO) Immediately after receiving these admonishments, _____
_____
_____
_____
An SSA must review _____ admonishment documentation and ensure that it is maintained in
_____ (see subsection 13.9., "Recordkeeping Procedures").

13.6.   (U) Renewal and Expansion of _____

(U//FOUO) If an agent seeks to obtain reauthorization for any CHS _____ after the   b3
expiration of the authorized time period or after the revocation of authorization or, if he or she   b7E
seeks to expand, in any material way, a CHS's authorization _____ the requesting
agent must first comply with the procedures set forth in subsection 13.2.2. (
_____ or 13.3.1. _____
and subsections 13.4. ("Documented Findings of _____
_____ and 13.5. ("Admonishments Related to _____

13.7.   (U) _____

(U//FOUO) _____
_____

- (U//FOUO) _____   b3
  _____   b7E

- (U//FOUO) _____
  _____

- (U//FOUO) _____

13.8.   (U) _____

(U//FOUO) _____
_____

- (U//FOUO) _____   b3
- (U//FOUO) _____   b7E
- (U//FOUO) _____
- (U//FOUO) _____
  _____

- (U//FOUO) _____

(U//FOUO) _____
_____
_____
_____

b3
b7

13.9. (U) Recordkeeping Procedures

(U//~~FOUO~~)   b3

_____ must be maintained for each CHS   b7
_____ At the end of each calendar year, _____ must report to the AAG of the Criminal Division and the NSD the total number of times that each FO_____
_____ as well as the overall nationwide totals. If requested to do so, _____ must provide the AAG of the Criminal Division or the NSD with a copy of the written authorization, finding, or instruction pertaining _____

14. (U//FOUO) Operation of Confidential Human Sources Involving Other Federal, State, Local, and Tribal Agencies or FBI Field Offices

14.1. (U) Joint Operations of FBI Confidential Human Sources With Other Agencies

(U//FOUO) Joint operation of a CHS takes place when the FBI and one or more other agencies operate an FBI CHS together in a matter of mutual interest to all agencies involved. CHS operations, while joint, must comply with applicable AGGs and FBI policies.

14.1.1. (S//NF)

b1
b3
b7E

(S//NF)

14.2. (U) Sole Operation of an FBI Confidential Human Source by Another Agency

(U//FOUO) The sole operation of a CHS by another agency occurs when an FBI CHS is temporarily turned over to another agency for operation in a matter of exclusive interest to that agency. The FBI, however, must relinquish responsibility for the CHS to the other agency and must have no role in tasking, paying, or contacting the CHS in connection with the other agency's investigation.

(U//FOUO) In order for an FO to turn over a CHS to another agency for sole operation by that agency, the CA or co-CA must submit a request for SSA approval that includes (1) the name of the agency, (2) the name of the agency employee who will handle the CHS, (3) the nature of the case in which the CHS will be used, and (4) the anticipated duration of the operation. In view of the potential liability concerns of maintaining the CHS in an open status, the CHS must be closed while being operated by the other agency. In rare circumstances, such as those that involve the CHS's intelligence value or potential to assist other FBI operations, the CHS may remain open for up to six months while being operated solely by the other agency. During the period that the CHS remains open, all administrative requirements must be completed, including Quarterly Supervisory Source Reports (QSSR), FOASRs, annual records checks, and annual admonishments. In completing the QSSR, the SSA must evaluate the nature and duration of the CHS's use by the other agency and determine whether the use is negatively affecting the CHS's value to the FBI, to the extent that the CHS should be closed. Although the FBI is not responsible for validating the CHS's information or operation during the period the CHS is out of the FBI's control, the CA must make reasonable efforts to periodically (at least every 90 calendar days) obtain information from the other agency regarding CHS payments and any information the other agency can provide that has any bearing on the CHS's productivity, reliability, and credibility. This information must be documented[   ]

b3
b7E

14.3. (U//FOUO) Joint Field Office Operation or a Confidential Human Source Operating Within Another FBI Field Office

(U//FOUO) A CHS may work jointly with two or more FBI FOs. If the CHS resides in, moves to, or works in, another FO's territory, the OO must notify the SAC (or designee) and all other involved FOs of the CHS's opening. The OO must also notify the FO(s) of the area of anticipated reporting, and the notification must be documented[   ]The CA and co-CA may be located in different offices if it will enhance the CHS's operational effectiveness. The OO is responsible for maintaining the CHS's file and, if the CHS is jointly operated, the other FOs involved in operating the CHS must file all reports of information received from the CHS, as well as any required documentation (e.g., payment information and receipts), to the OO's file. Similarly, each office must keep the other apprised of information affecting the FO's investigative programs and of any changes in the CHS's status. For information on making a payment to a CHS on behalf of another FO, see subsection 17.9., "Paying a Confidential Human Source."

(U//FOUO) If an OO has temporarily turned a CHS over to another FO for operational use in that FO's investigation, the FO using and tasking the CHS is responsible for ensuring that all communications pertaining to the CHS's operation (e.g., reporting, operational requests, payment documentation, and validation-related information) are promptly entered[   ]

b3
b7E

[   ]CHS payments made by another FO are addressed in subsection 17.12., "Payments to Confidential Human Sources by Other Field Offices." The FO tasking the CHS must also keep the OO advised of any information it obtains from the CHS that would affect the OO's investigative programs. During the other FO's operation of the CHS, the FO tasking the CHS must contribute to the OO's preparation of CHS QSSRs and FOASRs and ensure compliance with other administrative requirements, including annual records checks and admonishments. If the other FO tasking the CHS has used the CHS exclusively for a six-month period and is likely to continue this use, the OO must reassign the CHS to the other FO.

14.4. (U//FOUO) Operation of Confidential Human Sources in Other Field Office Territories

(U//FOUO) This subsection concerns CHS domestic operational travel, during which a CHS travels from one FO's area of responsibility (AOR) to another FO's AOR or from a foreign country to the United States to conduct operational activity. Examples of this type of travel include a CHS traveling from his or her assigned FO to another FO to support an investigation; a Legat-assigned CHS traveling to the United States to support an FO investigation; or an FO-assigned CHS who resides in a foreign country and is traveling to the United States in support of an investigation. See subsection 19.4.1.5., "Foreign-Based Confidential Human Sources Operational Travel to United States (Domestic-Operational Travel."

(U//FOUO) An SA seeking to conduct a CHS operation in another FO's territory must obtain prior concurrence from that FO's SAC (or designee), if practicable. If it is not practicable, the affected FO must be notified as soon as possible, but no later than five business days from the date of the operational activity. An FD-1040a "CHS Travel/ET Activity Request Form" (in

[ ] should be used to document the prior concurrence or post-operation notification of the affected FO. If the form is used, an "Information Only" lead is sent to the receiving FO for situational awareness. The use of an FD-1040a does not preclude informal oral or written contact between FOs to coordinate the CHS's activity. Regardless of whether or not an FD-1040a is used, the CHS's domestic operational travel must be documented

(U//FOUO)

15. (U//~~FOUO~~) Disclosure of a Confidential Human Source's Identity

15.1. (U) Principles of Confidentiality

(U//~~FOUO~~) Protecting a CHS's identity and relationship with the FBI is vital to the success of that relationship and to the integrity of the FBI's Confidential Human Source Program. Consequently, FBI personnel have an obligation to maintain the confidentiality of any CHS, which includes the CHS's identity and information received from or regarding the CHS that tends to identify the CHS. This obligation continues after the FBI employee ends his or her employment and after the CHS ceases to be a CHS.

(U//~~FOUO~~) Disclosure of a CHS's identity, including the dissemination of information received from or regarding the CHS that tends to identify him or her, may be approved only when it is legally required or absolutely necessary to achieve important investigative, public policy, or safety objectives. This principle must be at the forefront of every disclosure decision, even with regard to prospective disclosures within the DOJ and among task force partners.

15.2. (U) Disclosure Authority

(U//~~FOUO~~) Approval of the SAC from the office where the CHS is assigned is required to disclose the identity of a CHS, unless:

1. (U//~~FOUO~~) FBI personnel disclose a CHS's identity to another FBI employee who, in the performance of his or her official duties, has a need to know the identity of the CHS.

2. (U//~~FOUO~~) FBI personnel make appropriate disclosures to the DOJ when a CHS has been called to testify in a grand jury or judicial proceeding.

3. (U//~~FOUO~~) FBI personnel disclose a CHS's identity when required to do so by court order, law, regulation, the AGG-CHS, or other DOJ policies (see subsection 11.7, "Responding to Requests from Federal Prosecuting Office Attorneys Regarding a Confidential Human Source").

(U//~~FOUO~~) The SSA may approve the disclosure of a CHS's identity in response to operational or administrative requests that, by their nature, require disclosure of a CHS's identity, including those related   b3
                                                                                                                        b7E
Prior to
approving a disclosure request, the SSA, in discussion with the CA, should consider the necessity of disclosing the CHS's identity, its potential for undermining the confidential relationship developed, and whether the CHS should be informed that his or her identity will be shared as part of an operational or administrative request. SSA approval of the specific operational or administrative request serves as the authorization documentation to disclose the CHS's identity. No separate documentation is required for disclosing the CHS's identity in such circumstances.

(U//~~FOUO~~) No individual to whom disclosure has been made is authorized to make further disclosures of the CHS's identity without SAC authority, except when required by court order, law, regulation, the AGG-CHS, or other DOJ policies. Anyone making a disclosure has the responsibility to advise the recipient of the information that further disclosures or contact with the CHS is not authorized without the express consent of the FBI.

(U//FOUO) All approvals to disclose a CHS's identity must be documented in the CHS[   ] b3
[   ] b7E

15.3. (U//FOUO) Special Agent in Charge Objections to Confidential Human Source Disclosure Requirement

(U//FOUO) With regard to a required disclosure, the SAC may still determine whether an attempt should be made to assert appropriate administrative or legal objections in response to any subpoena, court order, or request bearing on the identification of a CHS. In matters involving national security and other situations, a request may be made to have the CHS's file reviewed in-camera ex parte by a judge, as appropriate. In certain circumstances, the FBI may refuse the disclosure of either the CHS's identity or the information provided by the CHS. This action could result in the dismissal of the pending prosecution and must be coordinated with appropriate officials from the FPO. Any decision to withhold CHS information must be coordinated with the appropriate FPO and documented in the CHS's[   ] b3
b7E

15.4. (U//FOUO) Record of Disclosure of a Confidential Human Source's Identity

(U//FOUO) Disclosure of a CHS's identity or relationship with the FBI, as defined above, must be documented and retained in the CHS's[   ] The documentation must contain the following information:

1. (U//FOUO) The specific information to be disclosed (e.g., the CHS's name and address)

2. (U//FOUO) The names, titles, agencies, or departments of all individuals who will have access to the information

3. (U//FOUO) The specific nature of the circumstances, request, demand, or order that generated the disclosure request

(U//FOUO) The SSA approval of a specified operational or administrative request serves as the authorization documentation to disclose the CHS's identity. No separate documentation is required. See subsection 15.2., "Disclosure Authority."

16. (U//FOUO) Administration of Confidential Human Sources

16.1. (U//FOUO) Confidential Human Source Files

16.1.1.   (U//FOUO) Creation and Maintenance of Confidential Human Source Files ☐

b3
b7E

(U//FOUO) ☐ is the FBI's automated case management system for all CHS records. All communications regarding the CHS must be entered ☐ unless an exemption is authorized in accordance with subsection 16.1.2.

(U//FOUO) ☐
☐ is responsible for oversight of these documents. ☐
☐

16.1.2.   (U//FOUO) Exemption From Creation and Maintenance of Confidential Human Source Files ☐

b3
b7E

(U//FOUO) Exemptions from entering communications ☐ must be supported by compelling circumstances and must be approved by the SAC, the AD of the division managing the primary program the CHS supports, the AD of the DI, and the deputy director (DD). None of these approving authorities may be delegated. An EC requesting ☐ ☐ and must provide the following, without providing any CHS identifying or classified information (additional guidance on completing the request EC may be sought from the appropriate ☐

1. (U//FOUO) ☐
2. (U//FOUO) ☐

    - (U//FOUO) ☐

b3
b7E

    - (U//FOUO) ☐
    - (U//FOUO) ☐ ☐
3. (U//FOUO) ☐
    - (U//FOUO) ☐
    - (U//FOUO) ☐ ☐
    - (U//FOUO) ☐ ☐
4. (U//FOUO) How intelligence collected from the CHS that is critical to the FBI's mission, such as thwarting a terrorist attack or other national emergency, will be evaluated and disseminated to other FBI components or outside the FBI.

(U//FOUO) The EC must set a lead to the appropriate ☐ requesting DD approval for the exemption request. The ☐ is responsible for notifying the CA of the approval or denial of the request. If the request is approved, the ☐ is responsible for permitting the CA or co-CA to

b3
b7E

initiate the opening of the CHS, including the limited submission required [   ] as specified below.

b3
b7E

(U//FOUO) Upon receiving the DD's approval, the CA or co-CA must complete all mandatory fields in the source's opening communication [   ] so that the CHS can be paid and to ensure that the QSSR and FOASR can be accurately completed. However, to protect the CHS's identity, [   ] has created standardized responses to be entered into each field by the CA or co-CA. The following is a list of the mandatory fields and the responses to be entered:

(U//FOUO) Standardized Responses for Source's Opening Communication

b1
b3
b7E

1. (U//FOUO) [   ]

2. (U//FOUO) [   ]

3. (U//FOUO) [   ]

4. (U//FOUO) [   ]

5. [   ]

6. (S//NF) [   ]

7. (S//NF) [   ]

8. (U//FOUO) [   ]

b3
b7E

9. (U//FOUO) [   ]

10. (U//FOUO) [   ]

(U//FOUO) [   ]

(U) Confidential Human Source Policy Guide

(U//~~FOUO~~) Standardized Responses for Source's Opening Communication

11. (U//~~FOUO~~)   b1

12. (U//~~FOUO~~) b3

13. (U//~~FOUO~~) b7E

16.1.3. (U//~~FOUO~~) b3 b7E

(U//~~FOUO~~)

16.1.4. (U//~~FOUO~~) b3 b7E

(U//~~FOUO~~)

(U//~~FOUO~~)

16.1.5. (U//~~FOUO~~) Confidential Human Source File Structure and Content

(U//~~FOUO~~) b3 b7E

must be maintained only in

1. (U//~~FOUO~~)

2. (U//FOUO)
3. (U//FOUO)
4. (U//FOUO)
5. (U//FOUO)

b3
b7E

(U//FOUO) Information [   ] must be scanned, if possible, and uploaded into the appropriate file [   ] Information or physical items that cannot be scanned (e.g., [   ] Documents containing [   ] or other information that may identify the CHS must be filed [   ] copies routed [   ] as necessary.

16.1.6.　(U) Properly Classifying Confidential Human Source Information

(U//FOUO) If a CHS's background information or the information he or she reports involves matters of national security requiring classification, that information must be appropriately classified in accordance with the *Federal Bureau of Investigation (FBI) National Security Information Classification Guide* [links to a SECRET//FGI//NOFORN document]. This guide specifies, among other information that must be classified, the following:

b3
b7E

- (U//FOUO) [   ]

- (U//FOUO) [   ]

(U//FOUO) All classified information must be maintained [   ] and must bear the appropriate classification markings.

(U//FOUO) Any information with a classification level above SECRET must be referenced [   ] via a general-purpose insert denoting the location of the higher-classified reporting or information.

16.1.7.　(U) Documenting Confidential Human Source Information

(U//FOUO) [   ] or has intelligence value must be documented [   ]

b3
b7E

(U//FOUO) [   ] The documents must be appropriately classified and filed in the relevant classified [   ] or unclassified [   ] and in the appropriate operational case or intelligence files.

(U//FOUO) Information provided by the CHS that is not intelligence-based or testimonial in nature must be documented [   ] is used to document:

b3
b7E

- (U//FOUO) [   ]

- (U//~~FOUO~~)   b3
                                                                                                    b7E

- (U//~~FOUO~~)

- (U//~~FOUO~~)
- (U//~~FOUO~~)
- (U//~~FOUO~~)
- (U//~~FOUO~~)

(U//~~FOUO~~)

16.1.7.1.   (U) Dissemination of Confidential Human Source Reporting

(U//~~FOUO~~) This subsection addresses the dissemination of CHS reporting that does not tend to identify the CHS. The dissemination of CHS reporting that tends to identify the CHS is treated as a disclosure of the CHS's identity and is addressed in Section 15, "Disclosure of a Confidential Human Source's Identity."

(U//~~FOUO~~) The dissemination of CHS reporting is encouraged and should be made available to members of LE, the IC, or tribal authorities with proper clearance if it is within the scope of their missions (see DIOG, Section 14). Disseminations are made through intelligence information reports (IIR) or other documents created for the purpose of sharing information (e.g., an LHM, an intelligence assessment, a bulletin, or another intelligence product). For documents not created for the purpose of dissemination, such as an FD-302 "Form for Reporting Information That May Become the Subject of Testimony" or an [redacted] the   b3
dissemination must be recorded on an FD-999, "Assistance/Dissemination/Liaison Provided to   b7E
Other Agencies." CHS reporting must be closely reviewed prior to dissemination and redacted to protect the identity of the CHS, unless the disclosure of his or her identify is justified and authorized in accordance with subsection 15.2., "Disclosure Authority."

(U//~~FOUO~~) Whichever dissemination method is used, the CA must document the dissemination of CHS reporting, including:

- (U//~~FOUO~~) The name of the person to whom and/or the agency to which the information was disclosed.

- (U//~~FOUO~~) A description of the information disclosed.

(U//~~FOUO~~) The dissemination record, which can be a copy of the disseminated document (e.g., a copy of the FD-999, IIR, or LHM), must be maintained in the [redacted] The   b3
dissemination must also be claimed as a statistical accomplishment [redacted] noting the   b7E
file and serial number of the disseminated information or a description of the information that was disclosed. In addition, disseminations from the CHS's file must be documented in the FOASR.

(U//~~FOUO~~) If the CHS's reporting was used in a court document and the activity meets the threshold for claiming an accomplishment, that fact must be claimed as a statistic on the

If the CHS testifies in a court proceeding, claiming a statistical accomplishment on the [REDACTED] is sufficient documentation. For reporting at levels higher than ~~SECRET~~, the electronic file location must be noted [REDACTED]

b3
b7E

16.1.8. (U) Retention of Confidential Human Source Files

(U//~~FOUO~~) The National Archives and Records Administration (NARA) has designated CHS files for permanent retention; therefore, records relating to CHSs must not be deleted or destroyed.

16.2. (U//~~FOUO~~) [REDACTED]

b3
b7E

(U//~~FOUO~~) [REDACTED]

16.3. (U) [REDACTED]

(U//~~FOUO~~) [REDACTED]

16.4. (U) [REDACTED]

~~(S//NF)~~ [REDACTED]

b1
b3
b7E

16.5. (U//~~FOUO~~) Criminal Justice Information Services Division/National Crime Information Center Query Alert Notifications (QAN) (Formerly "STOP Notices")

(U//~~FOUO~~) [REDACTED]

16.6. (U) Positive Records Checks and Concurrence to Operate

(U//~~FOUO~~) [REDACTED] the CA attempting to open the person must first obtain the concurrence of the FO SSA conducting the investigation. The concurrence must be documented [REDACTED] then the CA must document that fact, and the individual may be opened as a CHS [REDACTED]

b3
b7E

7.13. [ ] n addition, an FPO may have to be notified (see subsection 11.3., "Notification to the Department of Justice of the Investigation or Prosecution of a Confidential Human Source").

b3
b7E

16.7. (U) Field Office Annual Source Report

(U//FOUO) A FOASR is the FO executive management's review of a CHS's file. The FOASR is a critical tool used to assess the CHS for continued operation. The CA must provide detailed information regarding the CHS that is relevant to each topic and question in the FOASR. A thorough and complete FOASR enables the SSA, the ASAC, and FBIHQ to accurately assess the CHS's operation and provides subsequent handlers with all information pertinent to the continued operation of the CHS. The ASAC is responsible for ensuring that squads fulfill their validation duties according to the standards set forth in this section. In addition, ASACs are responsible for the completion and submission of FOASRs by their due dates. An ASAC cannot further delegate this responsibility.

(U//FOUO) The CA must complete the FOASR [ ] once during each 365-day period, based on the date of opening for the CHS. The FOASR must be approved by the SSA and the ASAC. The final approver must submit the FOASR [ ] If the CA is unavailable to complete the FOASR, the co-CA (who is an FBI SA and not a TFO) must complete the FOASR. If no co-CA is available, the SSA must ensure that the FOASR is completed in order for the FO to remain in compliance. The FOASR must be placed into the CHS's [ ]

b3
b7E

16.8. (U) Quarterly Supervisory Source Report

(U//FOUO) The SSA must prepare a QSSR for each consecutive 90-calendar-day period for each CHS file assigned to the SAs under his or her supervision. The initial 90-day period calculation starts on the CHS file opening date. The SSA must complete the QSSR review within 30 calendar days of the end of the CHS's 90-day cycle. The SSA must review all subfiles for each CHS [ ] the SSA must document what action has been taken with respect [ ] or must explain why no action is necessary. In addition, the SSA must consult with the ASAC [ ] and the ASAC's concurrence with the SSA's course of action must be documented in the QSSR. An acting SSA may not conduct QSSRs of his or her own CHS files. The acting SSA's ASAC is responsible for conducting QSSRs of the acting SSA's CHS files.

b3
b7E

16.9. (U) Annual Database Checks

(U//FOUO) The FO must conduct queries [ ] databases once during each 365-day period [ ] Other database checks (e.g., [ ] may also be conducted once during each 365-day period, if applicable to their reporting. All queries and their results [ ] must be documented in a [ ] and noted on the FOASR. The FOASR, including any [ ]

b3
b7E

(U//FOUO) The annual [   ] b3
b7E

[   ]

[   ] The results of these searches, if conducted, must also be included in the FOASR.

16.10. (U) Documenting Confidential Human Source [   ]

(U//FOUO) If an FBI employee receives [   ] on an individual whom he or she reasonably believes to be an open CHS, the FBI employee must request that [   ] conduct a [   ] query on the name of that person to determine whether the person is a CHS. If the person is identified as a CHS, the query will alert the agent assigned to the CHS to address the query with the agent requesting the search. The assigned CA agent must then document the information received to the [   ]

16.11. (U) Other Confidential Human Source-Related Deconfliction Checks

(U//FOUO) A TFO, an SA, or an IA may request the [   ] in his or her respective b3
b7E FO or FBIHQ division to conduct a check of CHS databases, including legacy CHS files, to determine whether an individual is currently or was previously an FBI CHS. The request must be in writing (e.g., an EC or a record e-mail) and must have prior approval from the SSA of the requesting TFO or SA. The SSA must evaluate the request to ensure that sufficient justification exists to search FBI CHS files and that the request is neither capricious nor an improper use of resources. The SSA must also ensure that the request is rationally related to a national security or criminal activity purpose. If the request is approved and there is a positive result, [   ] in coordination with the assigned CA (if any), must disclose to the requestor only the CHS-related information that is necessary to support the request's justification. The approved requesting document and any information disclosed on a CHS must be maintained [   ] to the CHS's file. If a search yields a negative result, the requesting document must be maintained in the [   ] file related to CHS administration.

16.12. (U//FOUO) [   ]
by Another Field Office or FBIHQ

(U//FOUO) Physical possession of a CHS's original paper file must never be transferred to any individual outside the FBI [   ] b3
b7E

[   ]

(U//FOUO) Should FBIHQ or an FO require another FO's original CHS file, in whole or in part, [   ] with SAC approval. [   ] shipping classified FBI information. For access to open [   ] the requesting SA must make a request to the CHS's CA. When access is granted by the CA, the OO's [   ] will create the appropriate role for the SA requestor.

(U//FOUO) SAC approval is not required for requests for the original CHS file from Validation Section (VS) employees handling CHS validation matters, and FOs are required to send the requested information. See Section 20, "Confidential Human Source Validation," for additional guidance.

16.13. (U) Requirements When a Confidential Human Source is Injured or Killed

(U//FOUO) When a CHS is seriously injured or killed because of his or her cooperation with the FBI, the FO operating the CHS must immediately notify the appropriate ☐ unit and operational unit. A communication explaining the details of the incident must be forwarded to the appropriate ☐ unit and operational unit as soon as possible.

b3
b7E

(U//FOUO) When a CHS is killed because of his or her cooperation with the FBI ☐

b3
b7E

17. (U//FOUO) Confidential Human Source Financial Matters

(U//FOUO) The FBI may compensate a CHS for services provided and/or reimburse his or her expenses incurred in furtherance of an investigative matter, including those occurring in a foreign country. All CHS payments are subject to FBI audit procedures. See the *Confidential Funding Policy Guide (CFPG), 0248PG*, subsection 3.13.

(U//FOUO) All CHS payment requests must be submitted [   ]   b3
[   ]   b7E
[   ] All CHS payments, upon issue, must be
immediately reconciled with corresponding payment requests [   ]

(U//FOUO) Certain fiscal circumstances require DOJ exemptions from statutes that would
otherwise prohibit the activities. The fiscal circumstances are delineated in the [   ]
however, the applicable statutes and the requirement for a DOJ exemption apply even if the
operation is a CHS operation [   ]

(U) The following fiscal circumstances require exemptions:

- (U//FOUO) [   ]   b3
- (U//FOUO) [   ]   b7E
- (U//FOUO) [   ]
[   ]

(U//FOUO) See the [   ]
[   ] section on fiscal circumstances for
additional details. This PG is used only as reference for the parameters and procedures for
seeking DOJ exemptions.

17.1. (U) Payment Prohibitions

(U//FOUO) Under no circumstances may any payments to a CHS be contingent upon the conviction or punishment of any individual.

(U//FOUO) In determining the way to classify a particular payment to a CHS as a service or an expense, the CA should not consider whether or not that classification might result in a basis for an impeachment at trial.

17.2. (U//FOUO) Field Office Funding for Confidential Human Sources

(U//FOUO) FO funding allocations for CHSs supporting programs in the Counterterrorism, Counterintelligence, Criminal Investigative, and Cyber Divisions, as well as the Weapons of Mass Destruction Directorate (WMDD), are managed by the operational desks and budget units in those divisions. CHS budgetary enhancement requests relating to those programs must be submitted to the appropriate operational desk or budget unit. Funding allocations relating to CHSs supporting the Intelligence Program are managed by the appropriate [   ]   b3
b7E

17.3. (U) Special Agent in Charge Annual Confidential Human Source Payment Authority

(U//FOUO) The SAC has a payment authority of [____] per FY for each CHS. This authority is automatically renewed to [____] at the beginning of each FY. In the event that the payment authority of [____] is expended prior to the end of the FY, the FO may request an enhanced payment authority of [____] An amount exceeding [____] may be requested if that amount is justified by operational considerations. Annual payment authority is independent of the approvals for aggregate payment authority and must be sought independently.　　b3 b7E

(U//FOUO) A request for enhanced SAC payment authority must include the following information:

- (U//FOUO) [____]
- (U//FOUO) The dollar amount of the additional payment authority requested
- (U//FOUO) Supporting justification for the amount requested

(U//FOUO) The request EC must be approved through the FO SAC and serialized into the [____] using the two- or three-letter subfile designation of the FO or FBIHQ unit with primary responsibility over the program the CHS reports on. The CA must not use any of the CHS's identifying information and may only identify the CHS by his or her [____] and all of its subfiles are restricted, the CA must use appropriate caution so as not to reveal the identity of the CHS in the body of the EC.　　b3 b7E

(U//FOUO) The request EC must include an action lead to the FBIHQ operational unit responsible for the oversight of the cases on which the CHS is reporting, with notice (via information lead) to the DI AD. The action lead must request FBIHQ approval (according to the approval levels set forth below) to continue to utilize and pay the identified CHS. The operational unit must review the operational benefits gained from previous payments to the CHS and evaluate the operational benefits likely to be gained if the enhanced payment authority is approved.

(U//FOUO) The operational unit must advise the requesting FO of the approval or denial of the enhanced payment authority in accordance with the above guidance. The operational unit must document its decision to approve or deny the FO's request in an EC to the FBIHQ and FO [____] The FO may not make any additional payments to the CHS until the FBIHQ operational unit has advised that authority has been granted for continued payment. The FO must also maintain the approval/denial response EC [____]　　b3 b7E

(U//FOUO) The EC generated by the operational unit for approval or denial of the enhanced payment authority must be signed at the approval level appropriate for the amount of the request, as follows:

(U) Annual (FY) Confidential Human Source Payment Approval Authority	
Authority to exceed the annual payment authority threshold of [____]	Requires operational DAD approval
Authority to pay a CHS between [____]	Requires operational AD approval

(U) Annual (FY) Confidential Human Source Payment Approval Authority		
Authority to pay a CHS between [ ] and [ ]	Requires operational AD approval	b3 b7E
Authority to pay a CHS between [ ] and [ ]	Requires operational branch EAD approval	
Authority to exceed the [ ] threshold, and each [ ] increment above [ ] within the FY	Requires operational DD approval	

(U//FOUO) Delegated authorities within the operational divisions must be documented, in advance, to the appropriate operational division subfile, as directed in DIOG subsections 3.4.3.3.1 and 3.4.3.3.2.

17.4. (U) Aggregate Payment Authority

(U//FOUO) When the total expenses and/or service payments (the aggregate/lifetime total) reach certain incremental levels, FBIHQ approvals are required. Prior to reaching the [ ] aggregate threshold, and at the additional thresholds indicated below, the FO must request review and approval to continue to pay the source past the approaching threshold. Aggregate payment authority is independent of the approvals for annual payment authority and must be sought independently. In accordance with the approval levels set forth below, all requests for authority to continue to pay the CHS must include: b3 b7E

- (U//FOUO) [ ]
- (U//FOUO) Total services vs. expenses paid by the FBI.
- (U//FOUO) Supporting justification for the continued payment of the CHS up to the next aggregate threshold.

(U//FOUO) The request EC must be approved through the FO SAC and serialized in the [ ] using the two- or three-letter subfile designation of the FO and the FBIHQ unit with primary responsibility over the program that the CHS reports on. The CA must not use any of the CHS's identifying information and may only identify the CHS by his or her [ ]   b3 b7E

(U//FOUO) The request EC must include an action lead to the FBIHQ unit responsible for the oversight of the cases on which the CHS is reporting, with notice to the DI's AD and the appropriate [ ] must request FBIHQ approval (according to the approval levels set forth below) to continue paying the identified CHS. [ ]   b3 b7E

(U//FOUO) The FBIHQ unit must advise the requesting FO of the approval or denial of the enhanced payment authority in accordance with the above guidance. The FBIHQ unit must document the decision to approve or deny the FO's request in an EC to the FBIHQ and FO [ ]

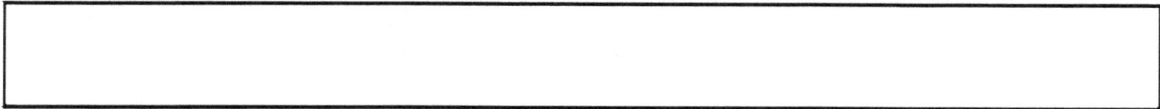

(U//~~FOUO~~) The EC generated by the FBIHQ unit for approval or denial of the continued payment authority must be signed at the approval level appropriate for the amount of the request, as follows:

(U//FOUO) Continued Confidential Human Source Payment Approval Authority	
Approval to exceed the [ ] and pay up to [ ] thresholds	Operational Division DAD
Approval to exceed the [ ] and pay up to [ ] thresholds	Operational Division AD
Approval to exceed the [ ] and pay up to [ ] thresholds	Operational Division EAD
Approval to exceed the [ ] threshold	DD
After DD approval at the [ ] threshold, the cycle resets back to the SAC for the next aggregate [ ] threshold.	
Repeat this process for as long as the CHS continues to receive payments.	

b3
b7E

(U//~~FOUO~~) Delegated authorities within the FBIHQ operational divisions must be documented, in advance, to the appropriate operational division subfile of [   ] as directed in DIOG subsection 3.4.3.3.2.

b3
b7E

17.5. (U) Confidential Human Source Payment Categories: Services and Expenses

(U//~~FOUO~~) Requests for CHS payments must distinguish between payments for services and payments for expenses. Although records of both types of payments must be turned over to the FPO attorney, as appropriate (see as reference [   ] [   ] it is critical that each payment be accurately characterized in [   ] the FBI's financial system.

(U//~~FOUO~~) A CHS obtaining intelligence from a subsource may be paid for reasonable services and/or expenses associated with that intelligence. At his or her discretion, the CHS may, in turn, pay the subsource from those funds. However, a CA or a co-CA is not permitted to submit a draft request to compensate or reimburse a subsource through the CHS.

17.5.1. (U) Services

(U//~~FOUO~~) Service payments are those made to compensate a CHS for the information or assistance he or she provided to the FBI. The payments must be commensurate with the value of the information or assistance the CHS provided to the FBI and may only be made after the services are rendered.

(U//FOUO) Service payments may be considered taxable income that must be reported to appropriate tax authorities. [redacted]   b3
                                                                                                        b7E

additional guidance, contact [redacted]

17.5.2.   (U) Expenses

(U//FOUO) Expense payments are those made to reimburse the CHS for reasonable costs incurred in direct support of an authorized FBI investigation or an intelligence matter and for which the FBI and/or the USG derives the primary benefit.

(U//FOUO) Only payments made by a CHS to legitimate and lawful vendors are considered CHS   b3
expenses. Payments that a CHS makes [redacted]   b7E
[redacted] are considered case expenses, not CHS expenses.
Likewise [redacted] are
considered case expenses, not CHS expenses.

(U//FOUO) The FBI's reimbursement of CHS expenses must be based on the actual expenses incurred, with the exception of relocation expenses, which may be based on an estimate of the expenses (see subsection 17.6.6., "Relocation"). Original vendor receipts or copies of vendor receipts must be obtained in order to reimburse the CHS or, if an advance of funds is obtained, to reconcile the advance. If a receipt is lost or missing, the CHS must attempt to obtain a copy. In circumstances where obtaining a copy of a receipt is not feasible, the CA must prepare a certification documenting the reason for the absence of a receipt (see subsection 17.7.2., "Vendor Receipts"). Once the actual expenses have been ascertained, the CA must ensure that the amount reimbursed to the CHS is reasonable based on the relation of the expenditure to the FBI matter it supports.

(U//FOUO) If, due to exigent circumstances and with prior oral SSA approval, the CA must use personal funds to pay a CHS or use a personal credit card or personal funds to purchase an item of value for a CHS (e.g. [redacted] prior to   b3
submitting the payment or reimbursement request through the [redacted] payment process, the   b7E
oral authorization must be documented in [redacted] as soon as practicable, but no
more than five business days from the date of oral approval. The CA must seek reimbursement in accordance with subsection 17.7.1., "Payment Request Entries," and subsection 17.6.5., "Equipment," if relevant. Under no circumstances may the use of personal funds, whether in an exigent circumstance or otherwise, exceed [redacted] Since this provision may only be used rarely, the authorizing SSA must ensure that the CA is exercising reasonable planning with the CHS whenever such a request is made.

(U//FOUO) Note that the purchase of equipment— [redacted]   b3
[redacted] —must be done in   b7E
accordance with *Confidential Funding Policy Guide (CFPG), 0248PG* (subsection 3.3.), and must be paid using case-related operational spending authority, not the CHS payment authority.

17.6.   (U) Rules Regarding Expenses for Meals, Vehicles, [redacted]

(U//FOUO) The expenses addressed in this subsection may be covered as CHS expenses under the circumstances outlined below. Expenditures must be closely monitored to ensure that the government obtains the primary benefit from them, and it is the responsibility of the employee submitting a request for payment and the supervisor approving it to ensure that the expense is reasonable.

17.6.1. (U) Meals Associated With Confidential Human Source Debriefings

(U//FOUO) Meal expenses incurred by a CA during a CHS debrief must be justified as an operational need. The full amount of the CHS's meal may be covered as a CHS expense, to the extent that the amount is reasonable and justified, based on the circumstances of the meeting. Government per diem rates may be used as a guide for reasonableness but are not determinative. Expenses attributable to the CA's meal, if justified, are covered by operational case funds. These expenses must adhere to government per diem rates. If they exceed those amounts, the CA must provide justification and obtain ASAC approval via an [   ]

b3
b7E

17.6.2. (U) Vehicles

17.6.2.1. (U//FOUO) Government Vehicles

(U//FOUO) CHSs are prohibited [   ] [   ] In addition, FBI personnel are prohibited from leasing or purchasing vehicles on behalf of CHSs. The parameters for supporting a CHS vehicle expense are set forth below.

17.6.2.2. (U) Vehicle Maintenance

(U//FOUO) If a CHS uses his or her vehicle in support of an FBI investigation, the FBI may reimburse the CHS for basic maintenance expenses (e.g., oil changes and tire rotation/replacement) in an amount reasonably proportionate to the vehicle's use in furtherance of the FBI investigation. Requests for maintenance reimbursements must be supported by vendor receipts. If it is not possible to attach the original vendor receipt to the draft request because it reflects the CHS's true name, a redacted copy may be provided to the draft office. The true-name copy must be maintained in the CHS's main file (see subsection 17.7.2., "Vendor Receipts"). The redacted copy must then be scanned [   ]

b3
b7E

17.6.2.3. (U) Vehicle Rentals

(U//FOUO) If it becomes necessary for a CHS [   ] in furtherance of an FBI matter, the CHS [   ] in his or her name and provide the vendor receipt to the CA. The FBI may reimburse the expense in an amount reasonably proportionate [   ] use in furtherance of the FBI investigation, and an advance of funds may be given to the CHS in accordance with subsection 17.8.3., "Advance Expense Payments," if he or she does not have funds [   ] After the rental receipt is provided to the FBI, the advance must be reconciled with the draft office.

17.6.2.4. (U) Vehicle Purchases

(U//FOUO) On rare occasions, with prior approval from the responsible DI DAD, the purchase of a vehicle that will be used primarily in support of an FBI investigation may be a reimbursable a CHS expense. The CA must submit a request that includes:

- (U//FOUO) [   ]

b3
b7E

- (U//FOUO) [redacted]   b3
                                                                                b7E

- (U//FOUO) [redacted]

- (U//FOUO) A statement that the CA has determined that the CHS has a valid driver's license.

(U//FOUO) At the FO level, the request must be reviewed by the CDC and approved by the SAC. The request must then be forwarded to the appropriate [redacted] which will coordinate   b3
legal review with OGC and approval from the appropriate operational unit.   b7E

(U//FOUO) [redacted] must advise the CA of the final decision on the request. If the request is approved, the CHS [redacted] in his or her own name. If the CHS uses his or her own funds to make the purchase, the FO may reimburse the CHS through CHS funds as a CHS expense. If the CHS does not have sufficient funds to make the purchase, the CA may obtain an advance of funds to be given to the CHS in accordance with subsection 17.8.3., "Advance Expense Payments." The CHS must provide the purchase receipt to the CA, who must then reconcile the advance with the draft office.

(U//FOUO) At the conclusion of the investigation [redacted]   b3
                                                                                               b7E
[redacted] even if requested to do so by the CHS. The fact that [redacted]
[redacted] must be discussed with the individual prior to purchase. [redacted]
[redacted] at the time of purchase is considered a service payment to the CHS. The individual must sign a CHS receipt for this value in accordance with subsection 17.7., "Payment Requests." The draft office must modify the original transaction in the FBI's financial system, and the CA must modify the original [redacted] to reflect the value of [redacted] as a service payment.

17.6.3.   (U) [redacted]   b3
                                                                                               b7E
(U//FOUO) [redacted]
[redacted] the individual's [redacted] costs may be covered as a CHS expense. This may be accomplished by obtaining [redacted] approval for CHS reimbursement for expenses incurred or, if the CHS does not have funds to cover the [redacted] expenses, by obtaining [redacted] approval for an advance of funds in accordance with subsection 17.8.3 , "Advance Expense Payments." The request must document the total [redacted] costs and the circumstances under which they were incurred, and it must be approved by the SAC and sent to the appropriate [redacted] unit, with copies of vendor receipts or invoices redacted, as necessary, to protect the identity of the CHS. The [redacted] must review the request, coordinate with OGC and the appropriate operational unit at FBIHQ, and advise the FO of the decision via EC. If the request is not approved, [redacted] must provide the basis for withholding approval. The request, with supporting documentation, and the decision to approve or deny the request must be serialized into the [redacted]

(U//FOUO) If reimbursement is approved, the FO may reimburse the CHS through CHS funds as a CHS expense. If an advance of funds is approved, the CHS must provide documentation of the [redacted] costs to the CA, who must then reconcile the advance with the draft office. In either   b3
instance, if the receipt contains the CHS's true name, a redacted copy must be provided to the b7E
draft office with the [redacted] and the original bearing the CHS's true name must be serialized to

[redacted] Receipts must be provided for [redacted] (see subsection 17.7.2., **b3**
"Vendor Receipts"). The redacted copy must then be scanned into the [redacted] **b7E**

(U//FOUO) Generally [redacted]
[redacted] that present after the CHS has been opened are not reimbursable as CHS expenses because it is difficult to discern whether [redacted] as a result of the CHS's cooperation with the FBI. Therefore, the CHS must utilize his or her own income (which would include any properly authorized service payments from the FBI) to cover these costs. However, the FO may request coverage of such expenses if justification can be provided that it is in the FBI's best interest to cover the [redacted] costs in furtherance of an FBI matter and that the CHS's cooperation with the FBI [redacted] The request must detail [redacted] costs, explanation of the way in which the CHS's cooperation with the FBI [redacted] and the operational necessity of covering the expenses. The request must be approved by the SAC and sent to the appropriate [redacted] where the request will be processed in the same manner set forth above for [redacted] expenses resulting directly from the CHS's assistance. The request, supporting documentation, and the decision to approve or deny the request must be serialized [redacted]

(U//FOUO) If a CHS is tasked to incur [redacted] costs in support of a substantive investigation **b3**
(e.g., as part of a [redacted] investigation), those costs should be designated as case **b7E**
expenses, not as CHS [redacted]

17.6.4. (U) [redacted]

17.6.4.1. (U) [redacted]

(U//FOUO) [redacted] **b3**
[redacted] **b7E**
payments as CHS expenses, in an amount reasonably proportionate to the use in furtherance of the FBI investigation. If it is not possible to attach a vendor receipt [redacted]
[redacted] because it reflects the CHS's true name, a redacted copy may be provided to the draft office and the true-name copy must be serialized into the [redacted] Receipts must be provided for this expense (see subsection 17.7.2., "Vendor Receipts"). The redacted copy must then be scanned into the [redacted]

17.6.4.2. (U) [redacted]

(U//FOUO) If a CHS does not [redacted] **b3**
[redacted] the CHS **b7E**
may be reimbursed for expenses [redacted] The FBI may pay reasonable expenses [redacted] to maintain the CHS's [redacted] The CHS must obtain the [redacted] and accept all liabilities associated with the [redacted]
[redacted] on behalf of a CHS, unless this is done in accordance with the *Confidential Funding Policy Guide (CFPG), 0248PG, subsection 3.29.5.* An additional justification occurs when [redacted]

_____   b3
_____ covered by substantive case funding.   b7E

(U//~~FOUO~~) The FBI may continue to reimburse the CHS [_____] as long as operationally necessary; however, ASAC approval is required every six months. The CHS must provide the original vendor receipt [_____] for reimbursement. If it is not possible to attach [_____] because it reflects the CHS's true name, a redacted copy may be provided to the draft office, and the true-name copy must be serialized into the CHS's [_____] Receipts must be provided for this expense (see subsection 17.7.2., "Vendor Receipts"). The redacted copy must then be scanned into the [_____]
[_____]

(U//~~FOUO~~) [_____] the CHS must pay any expenses associated   b3
with his or her [_____] These costs are not reimbursable CHS expenses.   b7E

17.6.5.   **(U** [_____]

(U//~~FOUO~~) The purchase of [_____] may be covered as a CHS expense if [_____] will be used in support of an FBI investigation or an assessment. The FO may reimburse the CHS through CHS funds as a CHS expense or, if an advance was paid, reconcile the advance with the draft office. The original vendor receipt for the [_____] is required (see subsection 17.7.2., "Vendor Receipts"). If it is not possible to attach the original vendor receipt to the draft request because it reflects the CHS's true name, a redacted copy must be provided to the draft office, and the true-name copy must be serialized into the [_____] The redacted copy must then be scanned into the [_____]

(U//~~FOUO~~) At the conclusion of the investigation, [_____] will remain the property of the   b3
CHS. The FBI may not recover [_____] from the CHS or assume responsibility for its   b7E
disposal. The remaining value of [_____] is considered a service payment. The CHS must sign a CHS receipt for the remaining value of [_____] and provide the approximate resale value and documentation thereof to support the expense. This documentation must be uploaded into the [_____] The draft office must modify the original transaction in the FBI's financial system, and the CA must update the original [_____] [_____] to reflect the remaining value of [_____] as a service payment.

17.6.6.   **(U** [_____]

(U//~~FOUO~~) If a CHS or his or her immediate family is in danger because of the CHS's   b3
cooperation with the FBI, the CA—in consultation with his or her SSA and [_____]—must   b7E
determine whether [_____] would be appropriate, based on the standards set forth in

[_____]

    b3
    b7E

(U//~~FOUO~~) [_____]

    b3
    b7E

b3
b7E

[redacted]

(U//~~FOUO~~) A CA may consider using case funds [redacted]

[redacted]

17.6.6.1. **(U)** [redacted]

b3
b7E

(U//~~FOUO~~) [redacted]

(U//~~FOUO~~) Government per diem rates should be used when determining expenses [redacted] With SAC approval, the CA may reimburse the CHS through CHS funds as a CHS expense or provide the CHS an advance if he or she does not have funds [redacted] The advance must be reconciled with the draft office [redacted]

b3
b7E

(U//~~FOUO~~) [redacted]

17.6.6.2. **(U)** [redacted]

(U//~~FOUO~~) [redacted] These expenses may be calculated in one of two ways: (1) by using estimates or (2) by using government per diem rates.

(U//~~FOUO~~) To use the estimate method, [redacted]

b3
b7E

[redacted]

(U//~~FOUO~~) Government per diem rates may be used in lieu of obtaining estimates [redacted]

b3
b7E

(U//FOUO) Whichever method of calculation is used, vendor receipts are not required to support the payment request. The payment request must be approved by the SAC (authority may be delegated to the ASAC). Thereafter, based on extenuating circumstances [   ] [   ] one extension of up to 90 days may be approved by the SAC (authority may be delegated to the ASAC). Any extension thereafter requires the approval of the appropriate [   ] unit.

(U//FOUO) [   ]

b3
b7E

- (U//FOUO) [   ]
- (U//FOUO) [   ]
- (U//FOUO) [   ]
- (U//FOUO) [   ]

(U//FOUO) [   ]

(U//FOUO) The CHS must initial the above advisements prior to receiving any funding from the FBI. Because this payment is based solely on the assessment conducted by the CA, the CHS does not have to document or explain how the payment was utilized. [   ] this fact must be documented in the CHS's [   ]

b3
b7E

17.7. (U) Payment Requests

17.7.1. (U) Payment Request Entries

(U//FOUO) Service and expense payments to a CHS are requested by submitting an [   ] which must include:

- (U//FOUO) [   ]
- (U//FOUO) [   ]
- (U//FOUO) [   ]
- (U//FOUO) [   ]
- (U//FOUO) [   ]

b3
b7E

b3
b7E

- (U//FOUO)

- (U//FOUO)

(U//FOUO) Standard justification paragraphs are not acceptable and should be rejected by the approving SSA and the certifying SAC (authority may be delegated to the ASAC). An expense reimbursement requires a specific breakdown of expenses (e.g. _____ and a justification for each expense. CA and CHS expense reimbursements must be clearly separated and justified _____ (e.g., CA meals exceeding the per diem, _____ the payment of a CHS expense, and other situations documented in the *Confidential Funding Policy Guide (CFPG) [0248PG]* that require specific SAC or ASAC approval).

b3
b7E

17.7.2. (U) Vendor Receipts

(U//FOUO) _____ the CHS must obtain vendor receipts for expenses incurred in support of an FBI matter. Prior to tasking the CHS to incur an operational expense, the CA must discuss with the CHS the requirement to obtain vendor receipts. The CA must note _____ on each vendor receipt and submit the receipts to the draft office with the _____ in order to obtain a reimbursement or to liquidate an advance. Vendor receipts must be scanned _____

b3
b7E

(U//FOUO) If the CHS cannot provide an original vendor receipt, a copy will be sufficient.

(U//FOUO) If a vendor receipt cannot be attached to the draft request because it reflects the CHS's true name, the CA must attach a copy of the receipt, with the CHS's name redacted, to the draft request. The CHS's _____ must contain the original vendor receipt bearing the CHS's true name. The redacted copy must then be scanned _____

(U//FOUO) For situations in which requesting a receipt from the vendor would endanger the CHS or disclose the CHS's relationship with the FBI, or in a rare instance in which a receipt has been lost, the CHS must advise the CA of the amount spent and the reason for not providing a vendor receipt. The CA must submit a certification _____ for the expense. The certification must contain (1) a statement that the CHS advised the CA of the amount spent, (2) the date the CA received notification, (3) the circumstances that precluded the CHS from obtaining or caused the CHS to lose the receipt, and (4) the reasonableness of the expense.

b3
b7E

17.8. (U) Payment Approvals

17.8.1. (U) Federal Prosecuting Office Attorney Approval

(U//FOUO) If an FPO attorney is participating in an investigation that is using a CHS who is expected to testify, the CA must obtain approval from the FPO attorney, in advance if possible, for payments made to the CHS. The FBI may obtain approval for a specific payment amount or a potential range of aggregate CHS payments that could be made for the duration of the investigation. If the CA proposes making payments for services and the FPO attorney objects, no service payment may be made until the dispute has been resolved through the AGG-CHS dispute resolution process. See subsection 1.5.1., "*Attorney General's Guidelines Regarding the Use of FBI Confidential Human Sources* and *Attorney General's Guidelines for Domestic FBI Operations* Exceptions and Dispute Resolution."

17.8.2. (U) FBI Field Office Approval

(U//FOUO) CHS payment requests require SAC approval. The final approver of the [ ] bears the responsibility of ensuring the accuracy of the payment request and compliance with all CHS policies, the *Confidential Funding Policy Guide (CFPG), 0248PG*, and other federal government regulations and policies (e.g., those on travel and procurement). The final approver, therefore, must sign as the "certifier," indicating his or her certification of compliance, before the [ ] can be submitted to the draft office.

(U//FOUO) In the event of a rare situation in which a payment must be made immediately due to operational or security reasons, and SAC approval cannot be obtained prior to making the payment, the SAC must be notified of the payment within 24 hours. The CA must document the notification to the SAC [ ] within 24 hours.

17.8.3. (U) Advance Expense Payments

(U//FOUO) The SAC may approve expense payments to a CHS in advance of the expenses being incurred for up to [ ] per payment, totaling no more than [ ] per FY. The payment request must document the justification for the need to advance funding to the CHS. Approval of an advance is appropriate in situations where a CHS is expected to incur significant expenses in connection with his or her operation, such as for operational travel. When funds are advanced, the CA must ensure that the actual expenses incurred by the CHS are supported with vendor receipts or, where allowed, CA certification (see subsection 17.7.2., "Vendor Receipts"). Based on the vendor receipts or certification, the actual expenses are to be reconciled with the advance of funds. After the CHS submits the vendor receipts and any unused funds, he or she must sign a second receipt that reflects the actual amount spent and any funds the CHS returned to the CA. The CA must ensure that the appropriate amount for the payment is reconciled [ ]

17.9. (U) Paying a Confidential Human Source

(U//FOUO) After obtaining the approvals outlined in subsection 17.7., "Payment Requests," and subsection 17.8., "Payment Approvals," the SA must submit the [ ] draft version [ ] to the draft office. The draft office will issue a draft check or deposit funds into the SA's government-issued account. The SA may withdraw funds from his or her debit card or cash the draft check to make the payment. If it is not operationally feasible to pay the CHS in cash, the SA may convert the funds to another form of payment, such as a cashier's check, a money order, or a nonreloadable debit card after documenting the justification

b3
b7E

b3
b7E

b3
b7E

for the alternate form of payment in accordance with subsection 17.7.1., "Payment Request Entries."

(U//~~FOUO~~) ☐   b3
                                                                            b7E

The request must (1) be in writing, (2) provide justification ☐ and (3) be approved by the SSA of the squad with oversight for the CHS and the ☐ supervisor. This communication must be retained in the CHS's ☐

(U//~~FOUO~~) In the event of extraordinary circumstances that must be documented in the CHS's   b3
file and approved by the SAC, ☐ The request must (1) be in writing,   b7E
(2) provide justification ☐ and (3) be retained, along with the SAC's
approval, in the ☐

(U//~~FOUO~~) ☐

The receipt must be retained in the ☐

(U//~~FOUO~~) If it becomes necessary ☐   b3
                                                                            b7E

the SA is unable to meet with the CHS (e.g., if the CHS moved out of the area and the SA does not have the CHS's contact information), the SA must initial the modifications to the CHS's receipt and document that he or she was unable to reach the CHS prior to submitting the CHS's receipt to the draft office and scanning ☐

(U//~~FOUO~~) ☐ the FBI agent or other government official must advise the CHS that the monies may be taxable income and must be reported to appropriate tax authorities. An SA must not provide tax advice to the CHS, but should instruct the CHS to contact a tax consultant (of the CHS's choosing) for tax advice if he or she has any questions. The advisement that the payment may be taxable income must be documented in the ☐

(U//~~FOUO~~) The SA must make reasonable efforts to ensure that the CHS ☐   b3
                                                                            b7E

(U//~~FOUO~~) If, for operational or security reasons, ☐

documented in the CHS's CE subfile. The CHS must provide the SA with same-day written acknowledgment of receipt of the payment. ☐

---

[8] (U) A typed name constitutes a signature in this circumstance.

b3
b7E

The prior SSA approval for the use of ▓▓▓ and the basis for its use must be documented in the CHS's ▓▓▓ If the CHS sends the payment receipt acknowledgement ▓▓▓

(U//FOUO) ▓▓▓ requires prior approval from the SAC and the appropriate ▓ unit, and it must be documented to the ▓▓▓

17.10. (U) Supervisory Special Agent Financial Audit of Payments

(U//FOUO) In preparing the QSSR for a review period in which a CHS has been paid, the SSA must ensure that the following requirements have been documented in the CHS's CE subfile:

- (U//FOUO) Payment request(s) specify the amount of money attributed to each program (criminal, cyber, counterterrorism, or counterintelligence) supported by the CHS.

- (U//FOUO) Approval(s) for payment(s) to the CHS were documented ▓▓▓

b3
b7E

- (U//FOUO) The payment receipt(s) were signed by an FBI SA and another SA or other government official, unless waiver(s) were granted (see subsection 17.9., "Paying a Confidential Human Source").

- (U//FOUO) Receipt(s) were signed and dated by the CHS at the time of payment.

- (U//FOUO) The period(s) covered were indicated on the receipt(s) and match the ▓▓▓

- (U//FOUO) Receipt(s) appropriately distinguish whether payment(s) were for services or expenses.

- (U//FOUO) The CHS initialed the tax advisement for all service payments.

- (U//FOUO) All CHS payments were documented in the ▓▓▓ and have been reconciled.

- (U//FOUO) Annual and aggregate payment authorities have not been exceeded.

17.11. (U) Acceptable Uses ▓▓▓

(U//FOUO) ▓▓▓ therefore, there is a need for consistency in language across the FBI. Accordingly, ▓▓▓ The "Mandatory" language must be used, as written, ▓▓▓ and the "If Applicable" language must be used, as written, in situations in which it is appropriate. Any omission of mandatory language, modification of "Mandatory" or "If Applicable" language, or addition of language not provided requires OGC approval, which ▓▓▓ will coordinate. OGC approval of language modification must be sought prior to presenting ▓▓▓ to the CHS for signature. OGC/CDC review is not required if ▓▓▓ is drafted in accordance with the preapproved language. If no modifications of the provided language have been made, see the following paragraph for the approval process.

b3
b7E

(U//FOUO) _____ must be approved by the SAC and then by the appropriate DI SC, the FD, and the operational division SC, as coordinated by the _____ before being presented to the CHS for signature. The CA must prepare an EC containing justification for _____ route that communication _____ for SAC approval. If applicable, coordination with the FPO participating in the conduct of an investigation or a prosecution that is utilizing the CHS is required prior to SAC approval. If approved, the package (i.e., _____ and SAC approval) must then be submitted to the appropriate _____ with an action lead in Sentinel. The _____ must review and coordinate the approval of _____ through the appropriate operational unit, the FD, and the DI SC. The approved _____ will be forwarded by the _____ unit to the FO who must be the CA, the co-CA, or another SA identified _____

(U//FOUO) Upon receipt of the FBIHQ-approved and _____ (i.e., the CA, the co-CA, or another SA, _____ must present _____ and subsequently provide the _____ to the COR's FO _____ to be scanned into the _____ The hard copy must be retained _____ If the signed agreement is routed or otherwise internally disseminated _____ _____

(U//FOUO) In order to pay the CHS _____ _____ that clearly documents the information and/or assistance provided that warrants the dollar amount identified in the agreement. The CHS cannot be paid more or less than the contracted amount by the FO or by any other FO utilizing the CHS. If a CHS does not provide the information/assistance that warrants the dollar amount, the agreement must be terminated or modified in accordance with subsection 17.11.1, "Modification, Expiration, Renewal, and Termination of Service Agreements."

(U//FOUO) The SAC must review all CHS _____ every six months to determine whether _____ may continue for another six months. Review criteria must include whether an operational need for an _____ still exists and, if service payments are included, whether the amount listed is commensurate with the services being provided. The SAC review must be acknowledged in writing and placed into _____ terminate within 12 months of the CHS's signature _____ unless extended in accordance with subsection 17.11.1.

(U//FOUO) _____ is between the CHS and the FBI, not between the CHS and an FO; therefore, any FO utilizing a CHS _____ must abide by the terms _____ The SAC is responsible for ensuring compliance with the terms _____ the termination _____

(U//FOUO) Approval _____ does not provide an enhancement of annual or aggregate payment authorities. These authorities must be requested separately, as noted in subsection 17.3, "Special Agent in Charge Annual Confidential Human Source Payment Authority," and subsection 17.4, "Aggregate Payment Authority."

(U//FOUO) CAs must consider that _____ _____ _____ award. The information and assistance provided during the time period for which a

CHS [redacted]   b3
                                                                        b7E

[redacted]

17.11.1. (U) [redacted]

(U//FOUO) An FO is prohibited from making modifications [redacted] after it has been approved at FBIHQ. However, a modification request may be submitted using the same process required for initial approvals.

(U//FOUO) [redacted] expires 12 months from the date of acceptance (i.e., the date of the CHS's signature). If the FO deems it feasible to continue [redacted] it must submit a renewal request using the same process required for an initial approval.

(U//FOUO) If an FO decides to terminate [redacted] prior to its expiration, and a   b3
payment is due to the CHS [redacted] the termination must be documented and   b7E
initialed on the CHS receipt for the last service payment under the terms [redacted] If the
CHS is not due to be paid [redacted] must be terminated via a
letter signed by the SAC, with a copy sent to the [redacted]

(U//FOUO) If the CHS decides to [redacted] the CHS must provide written notice. This requirement must be included [redacted] Documentation noting the CHS's termination must be placed in the [redacted]

17.12. (U) Payments to Confidential Human Sources by Other Field Offices

(U//FOUO) To ensure that annual or aggregate payments do not exceed the payment authorities (see subsection 17.2., "Field Office Funding for Confidential Human Sources," subsection 17.3., "Special Agent in Charge Annual Confidential Human Source Payment Authority," and subsection 17.4., "Aggregate Payment Authority"), all payments made to a CHS by another FO must be coordinated with the OO. Payments may be made by either the OO or the FO that utilized the CHS. The payment authority, however, always remains the responsibility of the OO.   b3
All payments must be documented in the [redacted]   b7E

17.13. (U) [redacted]

(U//FOUO) An SAC may approve [redacted] in limited circumstances, such as when there are facts to indicate that a CHS whose assistance justifies a service payment [redacted] Prior to submitting a request to [redacted] the CA must ensure that the CHS [redacted] SAC approval must be granted before [redacted]

[redacted] An FO must not use CHS [redacted]

[redacted]

(U//FOUO) [redacted] must be documented by a vendor receipt in order for the CA to be reimbursed or obtain an advance.

(U//FOUO) [redacted] a written payment receipt must still be executed in accordance with subsection 17.9., "Paying a Confidential Human Source."

17.14. (U) Lump-Sum Payments

(U//FOUO) A CA may request a lump-sum payment for a CHS at the conclusion of any investigation in which the CHS has made significant contributions to FBI investigative matters or at the conclusion of the CHS's operation for the FBI. The CHS may only receive a lump-sum payment for information or assistance for which he or she was not previously compensated. This does not preclude a CHS from receiving a lump-sum payment for the same investigation for which he or she previously received service payments; however, the lump-sum payment must compensate the CHS for information or assistance not previously compensated.

(U//FOUO) Each lump-sum payment request must address the significance of the investigation and the CHS's contributions to it. The following information must be included in any request for a lump-sum payment:

- (U//FOUO) Title and file number of the case to which the CHS contributed information

- (U//FOUO) Details regarding the significance of the investigation

- (U//FOUO) Justification for the lump-sum payment (must be for assistance not previously compensated)

- (U//FOUO) [ ] attributed to the CHS's information or assistance that support the lump-sum payment   b3 b7E

- (U//FOUO) Whether the CHS suffered any financial loss (not previously compensated) as a result of his or her cooperation in the investigation

- (U//FOUO) The total amount of services and total amount of expenses paid to the CHS for the FY and during the investigation, and the total service payments paid to the CHS for the investigation(s) described in the first point above

- (U//FOUO) Whether the assigned FPO concurs with the payment (if the CHS is to testify or has testified)

- (U//FOUO) The value of seized or forfeited property obtained as a result of the CHS's cooperation and whether the CHS has received or would be nominated for an award or nominated for a payment resulting from forfeited assets

- (U//FOUO) Whether the CHS has or will receive any payment for services or expenses from any other LE agency/agencies in connection with the information or services that he or she provided to the FBI

(U//FOUO) The lump-sum payment request must be approved by the SAC. A lump-sum payment must be paid from the FO's budget, subject to the SAC's annual payment authority. If the payment is within the SAC's payment authority, but the FO's budget has insufficient funding, an enhancement request must be coordinated through the budget unit of the appropriate operational unit (see subsection 17.2., "Field Office Funding for Confidential Human Sources").

(U//FOUO) A lump-sum payment request that exceeds the SAC's annual authority and/or one of the aggregate [ ] incremental thresholds must be submitted to the appropriate FBIHQ   b3 b7E
operational unit for approval in accordance with subsection 17.3., "Special Agent in Charge Annual Confidential Human Source Payment Authority." The operational unit is responsible for evaluating the amount of the requested lump-sum payment against the operational benefit

provided by the CHS's assistance. Operational unit recommendations must be approved at the appropriate authority level within the respective FBIHQ divisions, as stated in the *Confidential Funding Policy Guide (CFPG), 0248PG*, Section 2 (see portions on confidential case fund payments). The operational unit must advise the FO and notify the appropriate ⬚ unit of the decision rendered on the request.   b3
                                                                  b7E

17.15. (U) Rewards

17.15.1. (U) Rewards Offered by Entities Outside the FBI

(U//FOUO) A CHS may accept rewards from another entity offered as a result of his or her assistance. The reward must be documented in the ⬚ Approval to disclose the   b3
CHS's identity may be necessary in accordance with Section 15, "Disclosure of a Confidential   b7E
Human Source's Identity." If it is necessary for a CA or a co-CA to receive the reward on behalf of the CHS to protect the CHS's identity, the CA or co-CA must document the receipt of the reward and the transfer of the reward to the CHS. The CA's or co-CA's transfer of the reward to the CHS must be witnessed by the CA or co-CA ⬚ and the CHS must sign a receipt, as with any other payment, in accordance with subsection 17.9, "Paying a Confidential Human Source."

17.15.2. (U) Rewards Offered by the FBI

(U//FOUO) The policy on acceptance of FBI publicly advertised rewards is detailed in PD 0978D, *Publicly Advertised Rewards*.

17.16. (U) Forfeiture Awards

(U//FOUO) A CHS may receive an award based on a forfeiture even if he or she has already been compensated for the information and/or assistance that directly led to the forfeiture. However, the forfeiture award must be offset by any previous payments for information or assistance that led to the seizure, excluding expense payments.

(U//FOUO) A CHS may receive compensation of up to ⬚   b3
⬚   b7E

(U//FOUO) The forfeiture award request must be approved by the SAC and submitted to the ⬚ The EC request must include:

- (U//FOUO) A copy of the final judicial order of forfeiture or declaration of administrative forfeiture.

- (U//FOUO) The name and opinion/concurrence of the FPO AUSA involved in the operation of the CHS regarding payment to the CHS with forfeited proceeds, if applicable.

- (U//FOUO) The total value of the forfeited property.

- (U//FOUO) The amount of actual cash or residual proceeds, if known.

- (U//FOUO) The percentage of equitable sharing. (The sharing disbursement is based on the remaining funds after all expenses have been deducted, including forfeiture awards.)

- (U//FOUO) A detailed justification for the payment of an award, including the information or assistance provided by the CHS that directly resulted in the seizure/forfeiture of the property.

- (U//FOUO) Verification that the USMS has been notified of the FBI's intent to pay an award on the forfeited property. Forfeiture personnel in an FO are responsible for forwarding a communication to the USMS, documenting the FBI's intent to pay an award based on the forfeiture, and checking the award block on the sharing forms (DAG 72, Block F). The notification must be documented in the CHS's [   ] **b3 b7E**

- (U//FOUO) The total amount of services and total amount of expenses paid to the CHS for the FY in which the property was seized or forfeited and a brief justification for all service payments.

- (U//FOUO) Verification that the CHS was not previously compensated for the information or assistance that led to the seizure/forfeiture of the property for which the award is being sought. If prior payments have been made for such information or assistance, the communication must identify such payments.

(U//FOUO) If the forfeited property will be placed into official use, the appraised value will be used to determine the award. All other property must be sold, and the proceeds deposited by the USMS, prior to a determination of the award amount.

(U//FOUO) The CA or co-CA must submit the request for forfeiture awards to the appropriate operational unit upon receipt of the final judicial order of forfeiture or declaration of administrative forfeiture prior to any equitable sharing. The operational unit must evaluate the requested award payment against the operational benefit provided by the CHS and coordinate the approval of the request with the Forfeiture and Seized Property Unit (FSPU), FD.

(U//FOUO) The operational unit must prepare the approval communication for the FO, with notification to the appropriate [   ] unit and FSPU, and coordinate the necessary transfer of funding. **b3 b7E**

17.17. (U) [   ]

(U//FOUO) [   ] In order for the FBI to use that [   ] [   ] the appropriate [   ] unit must obtain an AG exemption.

(U//FOUO) [   ] and operational unit authority may be granted for a CHS to be compensated for services and expenses [   ] provided that all operational costs have been covered. Upon SAC approval and concurrence of the FPO attorney involved in the operation of the CHS (if applicable), the CA must submit a communication in accordance with the *Confidential Funding Policy Guide (CFPG), 0248PG*.

(U//FOUO A CHS may be paid [   ] however, [   ] **b3 b7E** Therefore, FOs must clearly document the termination of [   ] [   ] payments must be documented [   ]

17.18. (U) [   ]

(U//FOUO) With the exception of funds paid for goods and services rendered in legitimate business transactions, any money, [   ] [   ] must be turned over to the FBI. Disposition of such

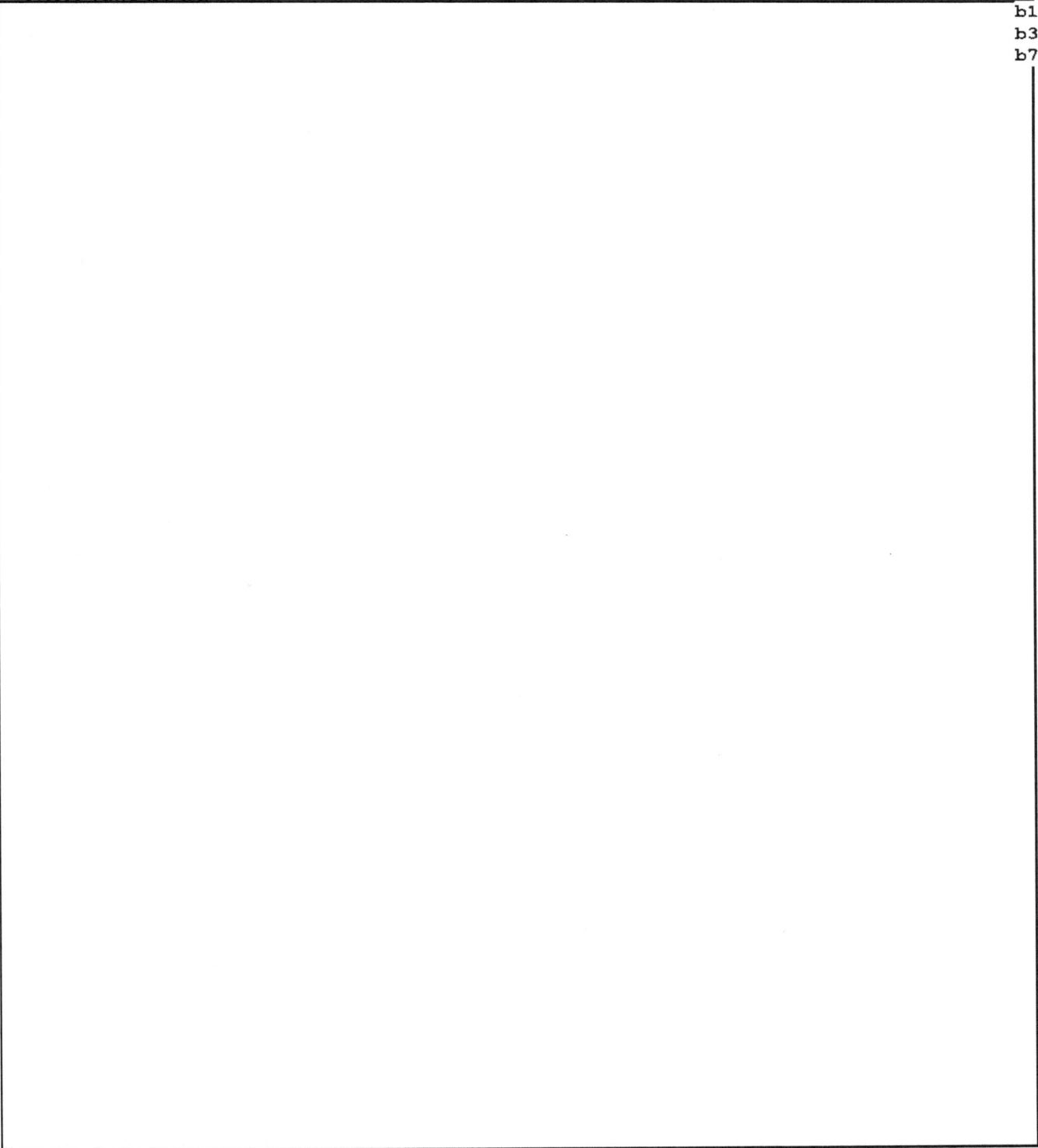

███ or gifts must be in accordance with the *Confidential Funding Policy Guide (CFPG)*, ████████, and with █████████

b3
b7E

17.19. (U//FOUO) █████████

b1
b3
b7E

b1
b3
b7E

17.19.1. (S//NF)

b1
b3
b7E

- (U) January through March
- (U) April through June
- (U) July through September
- (U) October through December

17.19.2. (S//NF)

17.20. (U) Payments to a Closed Confidential Human Source

(U//FOUO) Generally, a CHS may not be paid if he or she is in a closed status. In the rare event that a payment must be made either for services or expenses, the SAC may authorize a one-time payment to a CHS who has been closed. If more than one payment must be made to a CHS who

b1
b3
b7E

17.21. (U) One-Time, Nonconfidential Human Source Payments

(U//FOUO) The limits and requirements described in this subsection apply to non-CHS payments. With SAC approval, only one payment may be made to any individual who has provided information to the FBI in furtherance of an FBI investigation, but who has never been opened as a CHS for the FBI. For payments in excess of [   ] a communication requesting the amount desired, with a justification, must be submitted to the appropriate [   ] for approval. A non-CHS may only be paid for services rendered and/or expenses incurred by that individual, as defined in subsection 17.5.1., "Services," and in subsection 17.5.2., "Expenses." Payments to non-CHSs are charged to the CHS budget, using the appropriate case file number.

b3
b7E

(U//FOUO) Before approving a payment to a non-CHS, the SAC should weigh the benefits gained by making such a payment against the risks involved in not tracking the person as contributing to the FO's and the FBI's intelligence base and the risks involved in not providing protection to the individual's identity.

(U//FOUO) Non-CHS payments may not be used for the reimbursement of the expenses of agents or other LE or IC officials.

(U//FOUO) If payments are made to a non-CHS, the FO [   ] must open a file dedicated to tracking these payments in order to capture that person's contributions to the intelligence base and the amount of funds paid.

17.22. (U) Payments to a Nonconfidential Human Source [   ]

b3
b7E

(U//FOUO) CHS funds must not be used for the [   ] of an individual who has never been opened as an FBI CHS [   ] SAs are prohibited from opening these individuals as CHSs merely for payment purposes. SAs must use FO case funding or funding from the FPO [   ] for these individuals.

17.23 (U) Confidential Human Source Providing Money or Property in Support of an FBI Investigation

(U//FOUO) In order for a CHS to provide money or property in support of an FBI investigation, the ASAC must make a written finding that the acceptance of the CHS's money or property is necessary and appropriate for operational reasons. The written finding must include a determination as to whether the circumstances [   ] This written finding must be documented in the [   ]

18. (U) Closing a Confidential Human Source

18.1. (U) Closing Communication

(U//FOUO) When a determination has been made to close a CHS, a communication documenting the reason for closing must be included in the CHS's [   ] Those reasons are listed in subsections 18.1.1. and 18.1.2. Although more than one reason may exist for closing a CHS, the closed-for-cause category must be selected as the basis for closing if one of the reasons would justify closing the CHS for cause.

b3
b7E

18.1.1. (U) General Reasons for Closing a Confidential Human Source

(U//FOUO) A CHS may be closed because:

- (U//FOUO) Confidentiality has been unintentionally compromised.
- (U//FOUO) The CHS's cooperation has been completed.
- (U//FOUO) The request to operate the CHS has been denied by FBIHQ or another agency.
- (U//FOUO) The CA transferred.
- (U//FOUO) The CHS:
    - (U//FOUO) Has died.
    - (U//FOUO) [   ]
    - (U//FOUO) Is in poor health.
    - (U//FOUO) Has requested termination.
    - (U//FOUO) Has relocated or is unavailable.
    - (U//FOUO) Has been unproductive.
    - (U//FOUO) Is no longer in a position to report.

b3
b7E

18.1.2. (U) [   ]

b3
b7E

(U//FOUO) [   ]

(U) [   ]

- (U//FOUO) [   ]
- (U//FOUO) [   ]
- (U//FOUO) [   ]
- (U//FOUO) [   ]

18.2. (U) Closing Procedures

(U//FOUO) Upon closing the CHS,_____the CA and one   b3
other FBI SA, LEO, or person with a comparable position in a U.S. intelligence agency serving   b7E
as a witness, must:

- (U//FOUO)
- (U//FOUO)

(U//FOUO)_____and witnessed by the CA and the witness in one of the positions
described above.

(U//FOUO) In addition,

(U//FOUO) When a CHS_____the CA must <u>provide written</u> notification of the
closing communication to the ASAC (or via successor form_____ and a copy must be   b3
retained_____   b7E

(U//FOUO) When a CHS_____subsequent contact with the individual requires
special authorization (see subsection 18.3., "Future Contact With a Closed Confidential Human
Source"). In addition, a request to reopen a CHS_____requires additional
justification and supervisory scrutiny (see_____

18.2.1. (U) Delayed Notification

(U//FOUO) In the event that the CA or co-CA has determined that there is sufficient reason to   b3
close a CHS,_____   b7E

_____The decision and supporting justification must be documented in the

18.3. (U) Future Contact With a Closed Confidential Human Source

(U) Absent exceptional circumstances that are approved in advance, whenever possible, by an
SSA, an agent_____Approval for such contact must be documented in the CHS's_____
CHSs who were closed._____may be recontacted without prior approval.

(U) New information may be documented to a closed CHS file; however, the CHS must be
reopened if the relationship between the FBI and the CHS is expected to continue beyond the
initial contact or debriefing.

(U) To make payments to a closed CHS, see subsection 17.20., "Payments to a Closed
Confidential Human Source."

18.4. (U) Coordination With Federal Prosecuting Office Attorneys

(U//FOUO) If an FPO attorney is participating in the conduct of an investigation that is utilizing
an FBI CHS or the FPO is working with a CHS in connection with a prosecution, the CA must

coordinate (in advance, whenever possible) with the FPO attorney assigned to the matter regarding any decisions described in this section.

19. (U) ☐   b3
b7E

(U//FOUO) Unless specified otherwise in this section, all other provisions of this PG apply ☐

(U//FOUO) This section provides standardized policies for all investigative program areas related to ☐

(U//FOUO) The following authorities, to the extent to which they apply to ☐ govern the policies for ☐

- (U) ☐   b1
b3
b7E

- (U) ☐

- ☒ ☐

- (U) ☐

(U//FOUO) The aforementioned authorities differentiate between CHS operations in support of ☐ thus, different policy requirements are mandated   b3
b7E
for each type of CHS operation. In addition, FBI policy differentiates between the aforementioned investigation types ☐

[9] (U) ☐

(U) Confidential Human Source Policy Guide

(U//FOUO) Based upon the category of CHS activity, specific approvals, notifications, and documentation requirements apply. These categories are defined as follows:

b1
b3
b7E

- (U//FOUO)

b3
b7E

[10] (U)

b1
b3
b7E

- ~~(S//NF)~~

(U//~~FOUO~~) The CA or co-CA must complete an [   ] whenever the CHS activity falls within the above-listed categories, except for the

- (U//~~FOUO~~)
- (U//~~FOUO~~)

b3
b7E

- (U//~~FOUO~~)
- (U//~~FOUO~~)

(U//~~FOUO~~)

(U//~~FOUO~~)

b3
b7E

(U//~~FOUO~~)

(U//~~FOUO~~) An open full investigation is required for the FBI to engage in [   ] operations.

b3
b7E

(U//~~FOUO~~)

(U) Confidential Human Source Policy Guide

19.1. (U) [redacted]   b3
                                                                             b7E

19.1.1. (U) [redacted]   b1
                                                                             b3
                                                                             b7E

19.1.2. (U) [redacted]   b3
                                                                             b7E
                                                                             b1
                                                                             b3
                                                                             b7E

[11] (U) [redacted]   b3
                                                                             b7E

19.2. **(U) Required Approvals and Notifications** for ⬚⬚⬚⬚   b3
⬚⬚⬚⬚   b7E

(U//FOUO) The request for approval of an ⬚⬚⬚⬚

(U//FOUO) ⬚⬚⬚⬚   b3
                                                                                            b7E

- (U//FOUO) ⬚⬚⬚⬚
- (U//FOUO) ⬚⬚⬚⬚
- (U//FOUO) ⬚⬚⬚⬚

⬚⬚⬚⬚   b1
                                                                                            b3
                                                                                            b7E

⬚⬚⬚⬚   b1
                                                                                            b3
                                                                                            b7E

(U//FOUO) In exigent circumstances, oral approval and notifications may be sought. Such approvals and notifications must be documented using an _____ but no later than five business days from the date of the oral authorization.

(S//NF) _____

19.2.1. (S//NF) _____

(U//FOUO) In addition to the approval sought for an _____

(S//NF) _____

(U//FOUO) In approving the ☐ FBI officials must find that the ☐ is necessary to accomplish any of the following:

- (U//FOUO) _____
- (U//FOUO) _____
- (U//FOUO) _____

(U//FOUO) _____

(U//FOUO) _____

(S//NF) _____

b1
b3
b7E

(U//FOUO)

19.2.1.1.

(U//FOUO) The following approvals are required for

b3
b7E

- (U//FOUO
- (U//FOUO

- (U//FOUO)
- (U//FOUO)

(U//FOUO)

(U//FOUO) [   ] must be used to approve the [

b3
b7E

[13] (U//FOUO)

b3
b7E

19.2.1.2.   ~~(S//NF)~~   b1
                                                                                                   b3
                                                                                                   b7E

~~(S//NF)~~

(U//~~FOUO~~)   must be used to
approve the

                                                                                                   b3
                                                                                                   b7E

~~(S//NF)~~   b1
                                                                                                   b3
                                                                                                   b7E

19.2.1.3.   (U//~~FOUO~~) **Oral Authorization From the Department of Justice**

(U//~~FOUO~~) See DIOG subsection 17.6 for guidance on this authorization.

19.2.1.4.   (U//~~FOUO~~)   b3
                                                                                                   b7E
(U//~~FOUO~~)

                                                                                                   b1
                                                                                                   b3
                                                                                                   b7E

b3
b7E

(U//FOUO) The FBI, pursuant to

(U//FOUO) Requirements that fall into the second category are known as
requirements and may only be addressed under the policy for

b3
b7E

(U//FOUO)

(U//FOUO) [ ] is not authorized in support of a

19.3. (U) Criminal Investigations

(S//NF)

b1
b3
b7E

(U//FOUO)

(U//FOUO) This definition of

b3
b7E

19.3.1. (U)

(U//FOUO) The following

* (U) Authorizing CHSs to

•

b1
b3
b7E

b1
b3
b7E

19.3.2. (U)

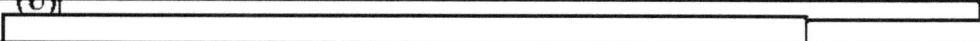

b1
b3
b7E

19.3.3. (U) _____ b3
b7E

(U//FOUO) The request for approval of an _____ must be initiated by the CA or co-CA using an _____ and must be approved in accordance with the below guidance.

(U//FOUO) The standard for approving the _____ is that it must be reasonably necessary to _____

b1
b3
b7E

(S//NF) _____

(U//FOUO) _____

b1
b3
b7E

(S//NF) _____

(U//FOUO) All _____ require:

- (U//FOUO) _____

- (U//FOUO) _____
- (U//FOUO) _____

b1
b3
b7E

- _____

- _____

b1
b3
b7E

19.3.3.1.   (S//NF)

b1
b3
b7E

19.3.4.   (S//NF)

b1
b3
b7E

(U//FOUO) An FBI employee must never authorize a CHS

(U//FOUO)

19.3.4.1. (S//NF)

b1
b3
b7E

19.3.4.2. **(U//FOUO) Approval and Notifications for**

b3
b7E

(U//FOUO) All [   ] conducted in support of a criminal investigation requires:

- (U//FOUO) SAC approval [   ]
- (U//FOUO) [   ]

- (U//FOUO) FBIHQ operational division AD (or designee) approval [   ]

b1
b3
b7E

(S//NF)

(U//FOUO) [   ] must be used to approve the [   ]

(U) Confidential Human Source Policy Guide

b1
b3
b7E

19.3.4.3. ~~(S//NF)~~

~~(S//NF)~~

19.3.4.4. ~~(S//NF)~~

~~(S//NF)~~

- (U//~~FOUO~~) SAC approval

b3
b7E

- (U//~~FOUO~~)

- (U//~~FOUO~~) FBIHQ operational division AD (or designee) approval

- (U//~~FOUO~~)

b1
b3
b7E

~~(S//NF)~~

(U//~~FOUO~~) [blank] must be used to approve the [blank]

---

[16] (U//~~FOUO~~)

b3
b7E

[17] (U//~~FOUO~~) See Footnote 16.

19.4. **(U) Policy Applicable to** [   ] b3
[   ] b7E

(U//FOUO) [   ]

[   ]

19.4.1. **(U) Documentation Requirements for All** [   ] b1
[   ] b3
b7E

19.4.1.1. (S//NF) [   ]

[   ]

(U//FOUO) [   ] b3
b7E

- (U//FOUO) [   ]

- (U) [   ]

- (U) [   ]

(U) Confidential Human Source Policy Guide

- (U) [REDACTED]   b3
                                                                             b7E
  [REDACTED]

- (U) [REDACTED]

(U) [REDACTED]

[REDACTED]   b1
                                                                             ╳b3
                                                                             b7E

(U//~~FOUO~~) [REDACTED]   b3
                                                                             b7E
[REDACTED]

(U//~~FOUO~~) [REDACTED]   b1
                                                                             b3
19.4.1.2. ~~TS//NF~~ [REDACTED]   b7E

~~(S//NF)~~ [REDACTED]

b1
b3
b7E

(U//FOUO) For example, if

b3
b7E

- (U//FOUO)

- (U)

- (U)
- (U)

- (U)

(U)

b1
b3
b7E

[18] (U//FOUO)

b3
b7E

b1
b3
b7E

(U//FOUO) The CA or co-CA must communicate

b1
b3
b7E

19.4.1.3.   (S//NF)

b3
b7E

(U//FOUO) For example, if   is selected as a category in the

- (U//FOUO)

- (U)

- (U)
- (U)

- (U)

(U) In support of the above, the completed [ ]   b1
                                                                   b3
                                                                   b7E

[ ]

(U//FOUO) The CA or co-CA must communicate an [ ]   b1
                                                                   b3
                                                                   b7E

19.4.1.4. [ ]

[ ]

(U//FOUO) Use of the [ ]   b3
                                                                   b7E

_____

[19] (U//FOUO) [ ]

[20] (U) [ ]

b3
b7E

(U//FOUO)

b1
b3
b7E

(U//FOUO)

b3
b7E

- (U//FOUO)

- (U)

- (U)

- (U)

- (U)

b3
b7E

(U) In support of the above,

(U//FOUO) As a general rule, an employee _____ is prohibited from

b3
b7E

b1
b3
b7E

19.4.1.4.1. (S//NF)

b1
b3
b7E

(U//FOUO) The CA or co-CA must communicate

b3
b7E

19.4.1.5. (TS//NF) [redacted] — b1, b3, b7E

(U//FOUO) [redacted]

(U//FOUO) For example, when [redacted] — b3, b7E

(U//FOUO) In support of the above, the completed [redacted]

(U//FOUO) This subsection does not apply to [redacted]

19.4.1.6. (U) [redacted]

(U) Whenever the CHS's CA or co-CA becomes aware that [redacted] — b3, b7E

(U//FOUO) For example, [redacted]

- (U//FOUO) [redacted] — b3, b7E
- (U) [redacted]
- (U) [redacted]
- (U) [redacted]
- (U) [redacted]

153

(U)

(U//FOUO)

(U//FOUO)

(U//FOUO)

(U//FOUO) The CA or co-CA must communicate

19.4.1.7. (U)

(U) Whenever the CHS's CA or co-CA becomes aware

(U//FOUO) For example

- (U//FOUO)

- (U)

- (U)

- (U)

- (U) [redacted]   b3
                                                                   b7E

(U) In support of the above [redacted]

(U//FOUO) [redacted]

(U//FOUO) [redacted]

(U//FOUO) In a circumstance in which a [redacted]   b3
                                                                   b7E

(U//FOUO) The CA or co-CA must communicate [redacted]

19.4.1.8.   (U//FOUO) [redacted]

(U) The purpose of this category is to track all [redacted]
[redacted] This information is collected as part of
the completion of the [redacted]   b3
                                                                   b7E

(U//FOUO) The CA or co-CA must communicate [redacted]

19.5.   (U//FOUO) Roles of the FBIHQ [redacted]

19.5.1.   (U//FOUO) Role of the Operational Division [redacted]

[redacted]   b1
                                                                   b3
                                                                   b7E

(S)

b1
b3
b7E

b1
b3
b7E

19.5.2. (U//FOUO) Role of the FBIHQ

b1
b3
b7E

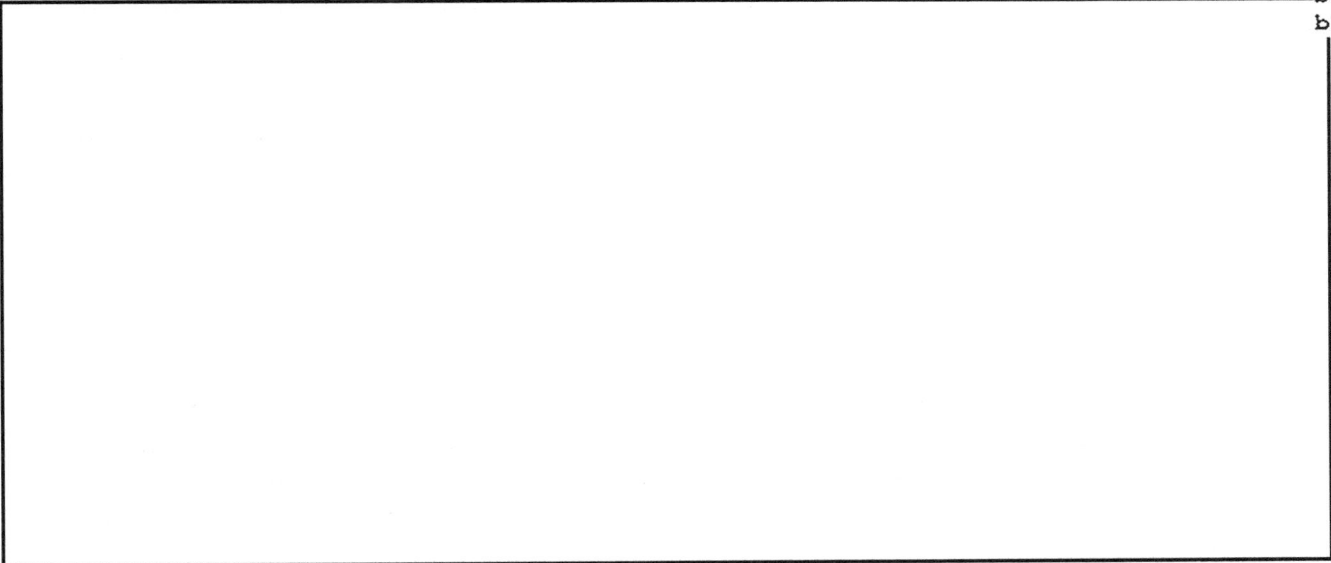

b1
b3
b7E

19.5.3. **(U//FOUO) Role of the** [redacted]

b3
b7E

(U//FOUO) [redacted]

b1
b3
b7E

(S//NF) [redacted]

(U//FOUO) [redacted]

- (U//FOUO) [redacted]

b1
b3
b7E

- (U//FOUO) [redacted]

(S) [redacted]

[21] (U) [redacted]

b3
b7E

19.6. (U//FOUO)

b1
b3
b7E

(U//FOUO)

- (U//FOUO)

b3
b7E

- (U//FOUO)

- (U//FOUO)

[22] (U)

b3
b7E

(U) Confidential Human Source Policy Guide

- (U//FOUO) _____ b3
  _____ b7E

- (U//FOUO) _____
  _____

- (U//FOUO) Coordinate _____ as needed.

19.7. (U//FOUO) Role of the _____

_____ b1
_____ b3
_____ b7E

- (U//FOUO) Review and cover _____ b3
  _____ b7E

- (U//FOUO) Review and cover _____

- (U//FOUO) _____

- (U//FOUO) _____ b1
  _____ b3
  _____ b7E

(U) Confidential Human Source Policy Guide

19.7.1. (U) [   ]   b3
                                              b7E

(U//~~FOUO~~) [   ]

(U//~~FOUO~~) Regardless of position, all [   ] must obtain approvals from either their [   ]

- (U//~~FOUO~~) Wherever the CHS policy mandates [   ]   b3
                                                     b7E

- (U//~~FOUO~~) Wherever the CHS policy mandates [   ]

- (U//~~FOUO~~) Wherever the CHS policy mandates [   ]

- (U//~~FOUO~~) [   ]

(U//~~FOUO~~) [   ]   b1
                                                     b3
                                                     b7E

19.8. (U) [   ]

[   ]

(U//~~FOUO~~) The opening request must be made in accordance with the procedures described in
Section 4, [   ] and Section 5, [   ]   b3
                                                     b7E

b3
b7E

(U//FOUO)

b1
b3
b7E

19.8.1. (U//FOUO)

(U//FOUO) Whenever an FBI CHS

b3
b7E

19.9. (U)

b1
b3
b7E

[23] (U)

- (U//FOUO)
- (U//FOUO)
- (S//NF)
- (U//FOUO)

- (U//FOUO)
- (U//FOUO)

- (U//FOUO)
- (U//FOUO)
- (U//FOUO)
- (U//FOUO)
- (U//FOUO)

(U//FOUO)

(U//FOUO)

(U//FOUO)

(U//FOUO)

19.9.1. (S//NF)

---

[21] (U) As noted earlier in the section, all provisions of this PG apply unless stated otherwise.

b1
b3
b7E

19. (U) [S//
b1
b3
b7E

[25] (U) The [_____] requirements are classified:

b1
b3
b7E

b3
b7E

(U//FOUO) If the [redacted] cannot be performed in person, secure communication protocols must be utilized in accordance with [redacted]

19.11. (U) [redacted]

(S//NF) [redacted]

b1
b3
b7E

19.12. (U//FOUO) [redacted]

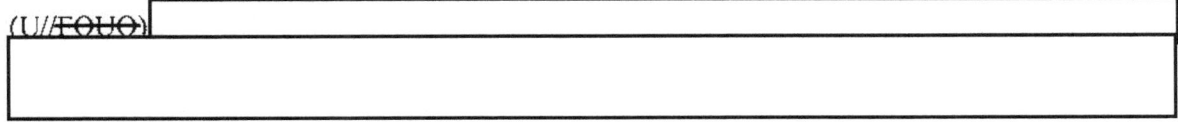

(U//FOUO) [redacted]

19.13. (U//FOUO)

S

b1
b3
b7E

19.14. (U)

b3
b7E

(U//FOUO) Approval for any CHS's participation in

19.14.1. (U)

b3
b7E

(U//FOUO)

19.15. (U)

S

b1
b3
b7E

b1
b3
b7E

19.16. (U) Special Circumstances

b1
b3
b7E

19.17. (U//~~FOUO~~) Use of an   b3
                                                                            b7E

(U//~~FOUO~~)

19.18. (U) Communications About a Confidential Human Source

(U//~~FOUO~~) Communications between FBI personnel

b1
b3
b7E

19.19. (U

b1
b3
b7E

(U//FOUO) For the purposes of

b3
b7E

b1
b3
b7E

(U//FOUO)

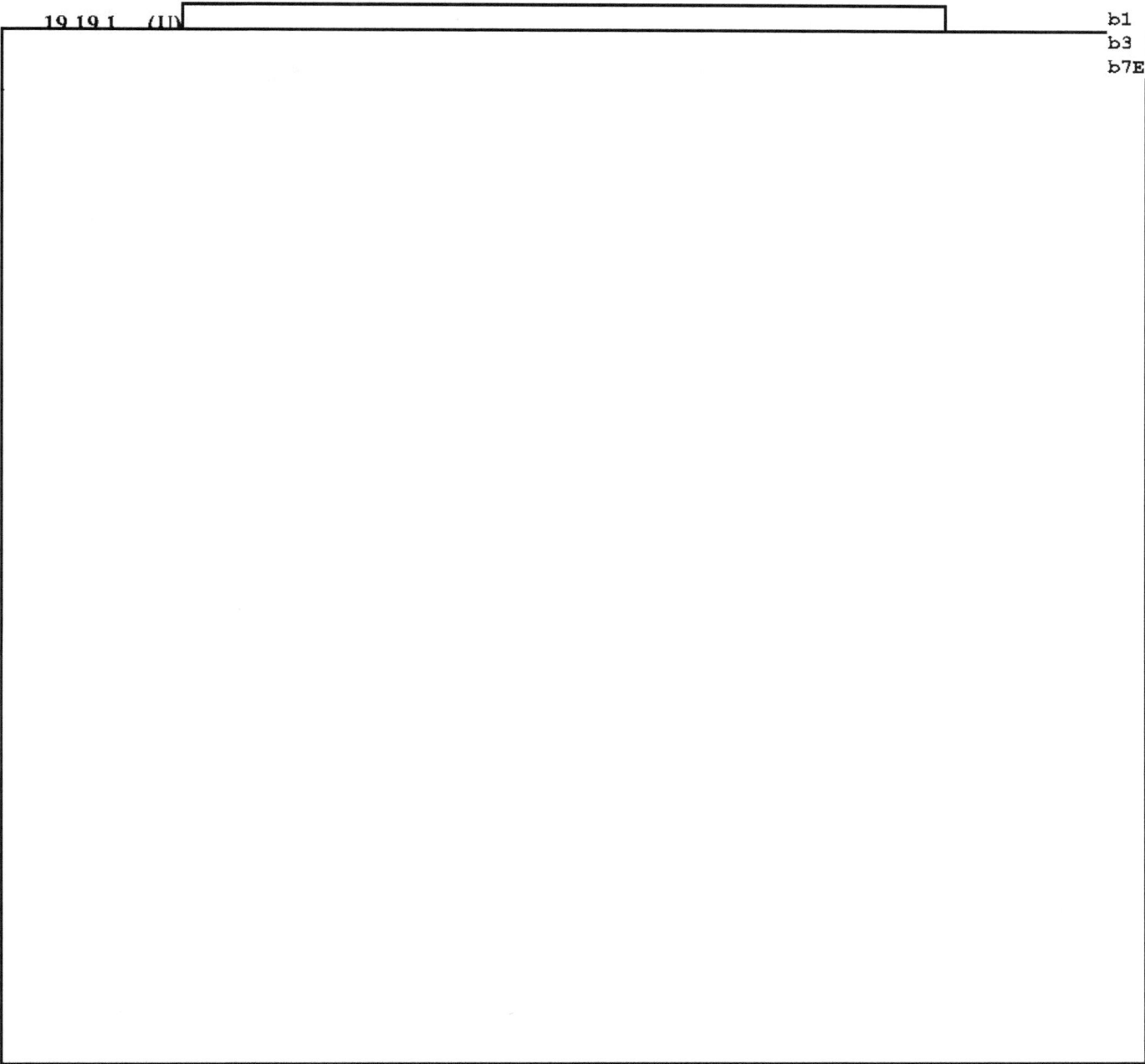

19 19 1   (U)

b1
b3
b7E

20. (U) Confidential Human Source Validation

(U) Until updated guidance on CHS validation standards policy is issued, please refer to the *Confidential Human Source Validation Standards Manual, 0258PG.*

Appendix A: (U) References

- (U)   b3
                                                                   b7E
- (U)

- (U)
- (U)
- (U)

Appendix B: (U)   b3 b7E

Confidential Human Source Reporting

(U) Overview of   b3 b7E

(U//FOUO)

(U) Requirements and Procedures for the Use of

(U//FOUO)   must be utilized to document and store   information obtained   b3 b7E
from a CHS.

(U) Requirements for Closing

(U//FOUO) When a source is closed,

will conduct a biannual review.

Appendix D: (U//FOUO) Acronyms

AAG	assistant Attorney General
ACS	Automated Case Support
AD	assistant director
ADIC	assistant director in charge
AFOSI	Air Force Office of Special Investigations
AGG	Attorney General guidelines
AGG-CHS	*The Attorney General's Guidelines Regarding the Use of FBI Confidential Human Sources*
AGG-Dom	*The Attorney General's Guidelines for Domestic FBI Operations*
AGG-UCO	*The Attorney General's Guidelines for Federal Bureau of Investigation Undercover Operations*
ALAT	assistant legal attaché
AOR	area of responsibility
ASAC	assistant special agent in charge
AU	Audit Unit
AUSA	assistant United States attorney
BOP	Bureau of Prisons
CA	case agent
CBP	U.S. Customs and Border Protection
CD	Counterintelligence Division

b3
b7E

b3
b7E

b3
b7E

CDC	chief division counsel
CFP	chief federal prosecutor
CFPG	*Confidential Funding Policy Guide*
		b3 b7E
CHS	confidential human source
		b3 b7E
CHSPG	*Confidential Human Source Policy Guide*
CI	counterintelligence
CIA	Central Intelligence Agency
CIS	Citizenship and Immigration Services
CJIS	Criminal Justice Information Services [Division]
co-CA	co-case agent
		b3 b7E
COM	chief of mission
CONUS	continental United States
COR	contracting officer's representative
		b3 b7E
CPI	Crime Problem Indicator [code]
		b3 b7E
CTD	Counterterrorism Division
CTS	Counterterrorism Section

DAD	deputy assistant director
DAG	deputy Attorney General
DD	deputy director
DEA	Drug Enforcement Administration

DHS	Department of Homeland Security
DI	Directorate of Intelligence
DIOG	*Domestic Investigations and Operations Guide*
DLAT	deputy legal attaché
DNI	Director of National Intelligence
DOB	date of birth
DoD	Department of Defense
DOE	Department of Energy
DOJ	Department of Justice
DOS	Department of State
DT	domestic terrorism
EAD	executive assistant director
EC	electronic communication
ECC	electronic country clearance
ECPA	Electronic Communications Privacy Act
ELSUR	electronic surveillance
EO	executive order

		b3 b7E

fax	facsimile	
FBI	Federal Bureau of Investigation	
FBIHQ	Federal Bureau of Investigation Headquarters	
FD	Finance Division	
		b3 b7E
FO	field office	
FOASR	Field Office Annual Source Report	
FPO	federal prosecuting office	
FSPU	Forfeiture and Seized Property Unit	
		b3 b7E
FTR	Federal Travel Regulation	
FY	fiscal year	
GS	General Schedule	
		b3 b7E

HSI	Homeland Security Investigations		
HSRC	Human Source Review Committee		
			b3 b7E
IA	intelligence analyst		
IC	Intelligence Community		
ICE	Immigration and Customs Enforcement		
IIR	intelligence information report		
			b3 b7E
IT	international terrorism		
JTTF	Joint Terrorism Task Force		
LE	law enforcement		
LEGAT	legal attaché (position)		
Legat	legal attaché (office)		
LEO	law enforcement officer		
LHM	letterhead memorandum		
LPR	legal permanent resident		
M&IE	meals and incidental expenses		
			b3 b7E
MD	Doctor of Medicine		

		b3 b7E
MOU	memorandum of understanding	
NARA	National Archives and Records Administration	
NCIC	National Crime Information Center	
NCIS	Naval Criminal Investigative Service	
		b3 b7E
NSB	National Security Branch	
NSD	National Security Division	
NSICG	*National Security Information Classification Guide*	
NSIG	*The Attorney General's Guidelines for FBI National Security Investigations and Foreign Intelligence Collection*	
		b3 b7E
OCA	Office of Congressional Affairs	
OCONUS	outside the continental United States	
OEO	Office of Enforcement Operations	
OGA	other government agency	
OGC	Office of the General Counsel	
		b3 b7E
OO	office of origin	
OTD	Operational Technology Division	
PCHS	potential confidential human source	

PD	policy directive	
PED	portable electronic device	b3 b7E
PG	policy guide	
PII	personally identifiable information	
PM	program manager	
POB	place of birth	
POC	point of contact	
QAN	query alert notification	
QSSR	Quarterly Supervisory Source Report	
RA	resident agency	
RCS	Records Collection System	
RFI	request for information	b3 b7E
SA	special agent	
SAC	special agent in charge	
SC	section chief	
SecD	Security Division	

SES	Senior Executive Service
SIA	supervisory intelligence analyst
SIM	sensitive investigative matter

b3
b7E

SSA	supervisory special agent
SSI	source sensitive information
SSIA	senior supervisory intelligence analyst
SSN	social security number
TDY	temporary duty [assignment]

b3
b7E

TFM	task force member
TFO	task force officer
U.S.	United States
U.S.C.	United States Code

b3
b7E

(U) Confidential Human Source Policy Guide

UNI	Universal Index
USAO	United States Attorney's Office
USCIS	United States Citizenship and Immigration Services
USG	United States government
USMS	United States Marshals Service
USSG	United States Sentencing Guidelines
VoIP	Voice over Internet Protocol
VS	Validation Section
WFO	Washington Field Office
WHO	World Health Organization

b3
b7E